A. THE CUILLIN HILLS AND BLAVEN, SKYE, FORMED OF TERTIARY PLUTONIC
ROCKS (GABBRO), FROM SOUTH-EAST

*Strathaird penninsula (middle distance) is composed of Jurassic strata overlain
by Tertiary basalt lavas and the nearer headland of Torridonian*

B. BEN MORE, MULL, A 3,000-FT. PILE OF TERTIARY BASALT LAVAS, FROM
NORTH-WEST

On right, below cliffs near Gribun, Mesozoic strata underlie the lavas

DEPARTMENT OF SCIENTIFIC AND INDUSTRIAL RESEARCH

GEOLOGICAL SURVEY AND MUSEUM

BRITISH REGIONAL GEOLOGY

Scotland:
The Tertiary Volcanic
Districts

(*THIRD EDITION*)

By

J. E. RICHEY, M.C., Sc.D., F.R.S.

with

Revision by

A. G. MACGREGOR, M.C., D.Sc. and F. W. ANDERSON, D.Sc.

EDINBURGH

HER MAJESTY'S STATIONERY OFFICE

1961

The Institute of Geological Sciences
was formed by the
incorporation of the Geological Survey of Great Britain
and the Museum of Practical Geology
with Overseas Geological Surveys
and is a constituent body of the
Natural Environment Research Council

First published 1935
Second edition 1948
Third edition 1961
Second impression
[with extended bibliography] 1964
Fifth impression 1975

1SBN 0 11 880401 4

FOREWORD TO THE SECOND EDITION

IMPORTANT ADVANCES IN our knowledge of the region dealt with in this volume have been made since the publication of the first edition in 1935. The principal sources of new information and interpretation are indicated by the additions to the Selected Bibliography, but this list is not exhaustive and references to further literature can be obtained by consulting the works mentioned. Further, in preparing this edition, advantage has been taken of the work of the Geological Survey in Skye during the years 1934 to 1938, the results of which are briefly described in the 'Summaries of Progress' for those years. The revision has been carried out mainly by Dr. J. E. Richey; but contributions on the Dalradian and Ordovician rocks of Arran have been supplied by Dr. J. G. C. Anderson, on the Upper Carboniferous and Mesozoic rocks by Mr. F. W. Anderson and on the Tertiary leaf-beds of Mull, etc. by Dr. J. B. Simpson.

In addition to acknowledgments made in the text for permission to reproduce certain illustrations, we would record our indebtedness to the Council of the Geological Society of Glasgow for the loan of the block for Fig. 23.

FOREWORD TO THE THIRD EDITION

Since the publication of the second edition of this volume in 1948 our knowledge of the Tertiary Volcanic Districts has been considerably augmented. Research has for instance gone on in Arran, Ardnamurchan and Mull and, most extensively, in Skye and Rum. New information is now available about the remote island of Rockall. Amendments and additions to the text have been made in order to incorporate results of new work, economic information has been brought up to date, and the sections on fossiliferous Carboniferous and Mesozoic sediments have been re-written on the basis of modern palaeontological knowledge and nomenclature. The Carboniferous and Mesozoic sections have been revised by Dr. F. W. Anderson. The rest of the amendments and additions have been made by Dr. A. G. MacGregor, who has been assisted by Dr. F. W. Anderson in relation to northern Skye and by Dr. D. I. Smith in relation to bibliographical references.

Six line-drawings have been modified (Figs. 1, 4, 9, 10, 11 and 13) and references to literature have been appended to appropriate sections of the text. These references include almost all the relevant publications that have appeared since the date of the second edition.

The revised text has the approval of Dr. Richey.

An EXHIBIT illustrating the Geology and Scenery of the district described in this volume is set out in the Museum of Practical Geology, Exhibition Road, South Kensington, London.

CONTENTS

LIST OF ILLUSTRATIONS

FIGURES IN TEXT

PLATES

A. GENERAL VIEW OF INFERIOR OÖLITE, BEARRERAIG BAY, NORTH OF PORTREE, SKYE, SHOWING COLUMNAR SILL AT TOP, *murchisonae* ZONE IN THE FOREGROUND

B. GENERAL VIEW OF JURASSIC ROCKS BELOW DUN CAAN, ISLAND OF RAASAY
1. *Great Estuarine Series.*   2. *Ledge at Position of Oil-Shale.*
3. *Inferior Oolite Sandstone.*   4. *Slope of Aalenian Shales.*
5. *Middle Lias Sandstone.*

SCOTLAND:
THE TERTIARY VOLCANIC DISTRICTS

I. GENERAL INTRODUCTION

THE ISLANDS and promontories along the western seaboard of Scotland are noted for their records of intense and prolonged igneous activity during early Tertiary times. At that period, some 40 million years ago, volcanic plateaus forming part of a continental region must have extended continuously along the western coast. By now, owing to prolonged denudation, vast amounts of the volcanic materials have disappeared and the broad pipes of former volcanoes are revealed, as well as still more deeply situated plutonic rocks which lie close to the old volcanic hearths.

Basic dykes belonging to various stages of the igneous period are arranged in north-westerly linear swarms which extend far and wide across the British Isles, from the Outer Hebrides and North-west Ireland to the Yorkshire coast and the English Midlands. The swarms provide direct evidence of the widespread nature of the igneous activity. On the other hand, the erupted products of the volcanoes have been in large part swept away or have sunk beneath the sea. Only isolated portions of the basaltic plateaus remain, and the underlying older rocks are again extensively exposed. The more resistant plutonic masses have escaped much of the destruction, and it is in their vicinity that the most illuminating records of the period are displayed in the rocks. The plutonic intrusions mark the positions of centres of igneous activity unparalleled in complexity and abounding in interest.

The Tertiary igneous centres of Western Scotland are situated mainly along the northern part of the Inner Hebrides and include Central Skye, the island of Rum, the western part of the Ardnamurchan peninsula, and Central Mull, with, farther south, the island of Arran in the Firth of Clyde. To the north-west, a hundred miles from the mainland and fifty miles west of the Outer Hebrides, a sixth centre occurs in the St. Kilda group of islands (Fig. 2).

SCENERY

In the Tertiary districts two main types of scenery are developed. The Tertiary lava-plateau has been eroded into hills with terraced slopes rising usually, as in Northern Skye, to 1,000 ft. or more (Fig. 3). The great plutonic masses form the high mountainous districts, with peaks 2,000 to 3,000 ft. in height. Within the plutonic districts the shapes of the mountains depend upon the kinds of rocks of which they are composed. In Central Skye, for example, there is a striking contrast between the rugged Cuillins, formed of gabbro, and the smoothly contoured Red Hills, which are composed of granophyre and granite. A lineated type of country is found in many areas, more especially in the lava-plateau of Northern Mull and Skye, and is due to numerous north-west dykes and lines of crush which have guided erosion.

Around the coasts high cliffs often mark the eroded edges of the lava-plateau, beneath which are often disposed Mesozoic sediments, which are well developed throughout the Tertiary portion of the Inner Hebrides. Superficial deposits,

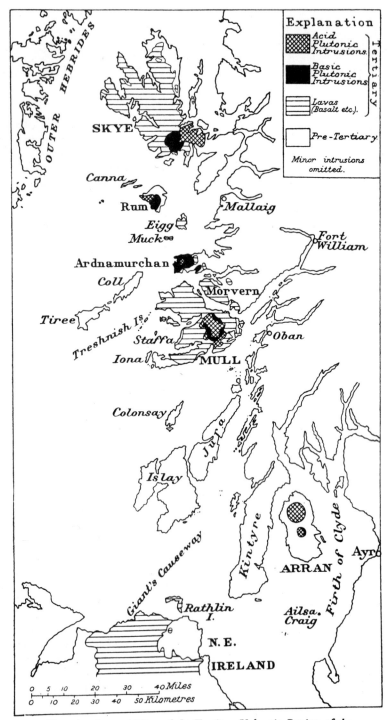

FIG. 1. *General Map of the Tertiary Volcanic Region of the West of Scotland*

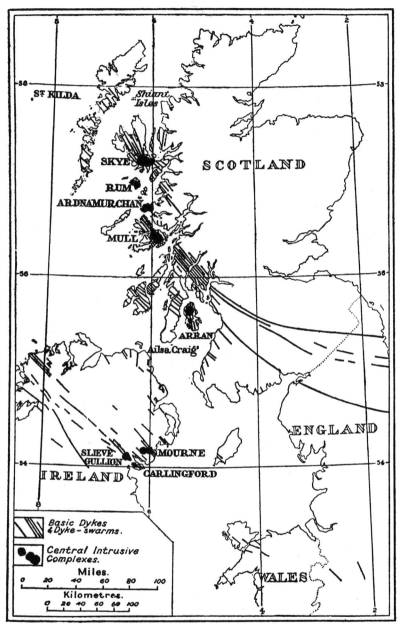

FIG. 2. *Map showing Distribution of Tertiary North-west Dykes in Relation to Tertiary Plutonic Districts of the British Isles*
[Rep. from ' The Geology of Ardnamurchan ', etc. (*Mem. Geol. Surv.*), 1930, Fig. 4]

such as boulder clay, hummocky moraines and river alluvia, also play a part in influencing the scenery. Spreads of raised-beach gravels form an almost continuous fringe between sea and hill, and peat extends along many of the valleys and the level terraces of the basaltic plateau. For the most part, however, the rocks are little obscured by overlying superficial deposits. The Pleistocene ice-sheet which swept westwards from the Highlands over the Hebridean region cleared away the surface accumulations of previous ages and left scanty glacial deposits in their place.

A radial system of drainage is characteristic of the mountainous tracts, such as Rum, North Arran, etc.; but many of the local rivers, especially in the plateau country, have followed north-west lines of weakness. There are also deeply trenched through-valleys, which belong to a time when the drainage of the islands formed part of a more extensive system. Examples are the Salen–Loch na Keal hollow in Mull and the Brodick–Machrie valley in Arran.

The coast-lines are dissected by extensive sea-lochs. There are numerous inland lochs, of various origins, of which a few examples may be mentioned. Loch Coruisk in Skye, 125 ft. in depth, is a rock-basin cut to a depth of 100 ft.

Broc-bheinn

FIG. 3. *View of Plateau-lava Country, Skye, to show Terrace-featuring Crossed by Hollows Eroded along Dykes*
[Rep. from ' The Geology of West-Central Skye, with Soay ' (*Mem. Geol. Surv.*), 1904, Fig. 8]

below sea-level by the erosive action of a glacier. The position of Loch Frisa in Northern Mull is due to erosion along a north-westerly line of weakness. Loch Bà, farther south, is an example of a moraine-dammed lake.

GEOLOGICAL FORMATIONS

The areas described in this memoir are chiefly composed of Tertiary igneous rocks, but many older formations are also represented, as detailed below.

RECENT and PLEISTOCENE

TERTIARY
{ Intrusion-vent Complexes
{ Plateau Basalt Lavas

MESOZOIC
{ Cretaceous
{ Jurassic
{ Triassic

PALAEOZOIC
{ Permian
{ Carboniferous
{ Old Red Sandstone
{ Ordovician
{ Cambrian

PRE-CAMBRIAN
{ Torridonian
{ Lewisian

OF UNCERTAIN AGE
{ Dalradian Schists
{ Moine Schists

Only brief accounts of the pre-Mesozoic formations are given, since they receive particular attention in volumes of this series concerned with other Scottish regions where they are more widely developed. The most extensive outcrops of Mesozoic strata in Scotland are those in the Hebridean area, and the formations concerned are therefore dealt with at greater length. The Tertiary igneous rocks provide the main subjects for description, since, apart from the far-extending north-west dykes, they are confined in Scotland to the region of the Hebrides and Arran.

REFERENCES
1819. J. MACULLOCH. *A Description of the Western Islands of Scotland.* 3 Vols. London.
1897. SIR ARCHIBALD GEIKIE. *The Ancient Volcanoes of Great Britain.* Vol. ii. London.
1901. SIR ARCHIBALD GEIKIE. *The Scenery of Scotland.* London.
1929. A. HARKER. In *Handbook of the Geology of Great Britain.* London (pp. 440–452).
1941. A. HARKER. *The West Highlands and the Hebrides.* Cambridge.
1949. G. W. TYRRELL. The Tertiary Igneous Rocks of Scotland in Relation to Iceland and Greenland. *Medd. Dansk. Geol. Foren.*, Bd. 11, No. 4, pp. 413–440.
1961. J. B. SIMPSON. The Tertiary Pollen-Flora of Mull and Ardamurchan. *Trans. Roy. Soc. Edin.*, vol. lxiv, pp. 421–468.
1963. M. J. LE BAS. On Dating the British Tertiary Igneous Province. *Geol. Mag.*, vol. 100, p. 379.

II. PRE-MESOZOIC ROCKS

WITHIN THE DISTRICTS of Western Scotland where the Tertiary igneous rocks
are so magnificently displayed, almost every Scottish formation of pre-Tertiary
age is represented. The rocks concerned belong to the ' floor ' over which the
Tertiary basalt lavas were extruded, and together with the lavas surround and
interdigitate with the succeeding volcanic vents and plutonic and hypabyssal
intrusions that now form the highest ground in Skye, Rum, Ardnamurchan,
Mull and Arran. The series of Tertiary intrusive complexes from Skye to Arran
cuts across not only many of the older stratified formations but also a variety of

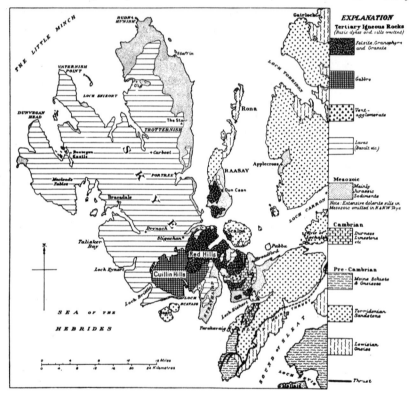

FIG. 4. *General Map of Skye*

geological structures. Skye, Rum and Ardnamurchan are situated not far from
the Moine Thrust, one of the most remarkable tectonic features of the Caledonian mountain-chain. Mull lies astride the Great Glen Fault, which divides
the Scottish Highlands into two dissimilar parts and was formed prior to the
Upper Carboniferous period, though movements along the extensive fracture
also took place during Mesozoic and later times (1946)*. Arran is traversed by
the Highland Boundary Fault. The association of the Tertiary volcanic districts
with ancient crustal displacements of such magnitude supplies a reason for the
variety of the pre-Mesozoic rocks encountered.

* Dates within brackets refer to References on p. 18.

1. Lewisian Gneiss: Skye, Raasay and Rum (*see* Figs. 4, 5)

The gneissic rocks of Skye (1910) and Raasay belong to three different structural horizons. In the north of Raasay and in the adjoining island of Rona the gneisses lie to the west of the great Moine Thrust, and are overlain unconformably by Torridonian conglomerates and grits. The main outcrop in Skye, bordering the Sound of Sleat, is separated from Torridonian rocks to the west by the thrust-plane itself, along which the Lewisian rocks have been moved bodily westwards, and are much altered in consequence. In the south-west of Sleat a few outcrops of gneiss, greatly affected by crushing, are involved in the Tarskavaig thrusts, to the west of, and beneath the Moine Thrust. Here, Torridonian rocks underlie thrust-masses composed of schists that are claimed to be lowly metamorphosed members of the Moine Series and have been termed the Tarskavaig Moines.

The gneisses of Raasay and of Rona are similar to those typical of much of the foreland of the North-west Highlands. They consist of hornblende-granulites, which are foliated and usually banded, with alternations of lighter, more feldspathic, and darker, more hornblendic, materials. The Lewisian rocks exposed for many miles along the Sound of Sleat include two different basic and acid groups, the one intrusive into the other. Both groups are much altered by the post-Cambrian (Caledonian) thrust-movements. Rocks with chlorite and epidote are prevalent, and porphyroblasts of hornblende and albite are locally developed (1955).

In the island of Rum hornblendic gneisses which were variously assigned to the Lewisian and Tertiary have recently been proved to belong to the Lewisian (1944a, 1945).

Basic dykes, pre-Torridonian in age, are plentiful in the gneiss of Raasay and Rona.

2. Torridonian: Skye, Raasay and Rum (*see* Figs. 4, 5)

Torridonian strata cover large tracts in Skye and its attendant smaller islands (1904, 1910) and in the island of Rum (1908). The general succession consists of lower shaly beds (Diabaig Group) and overlying red arkoses (Applecross Group). In South-eastern Skye where the greatest development is present there are 12,000 ft. of beds, and this thickness includes neither the base nor the top of the formation. The succession, briefly, is as follows, the higher beds taking on westwards towards the Tertiary mountain-tract:

Applecross Group 5,000 ft. { Red and chocolate arkoses, often false-bedded, with pebbles of quartzite, quartz-felsite, etc.

Diabaig Group 7,000 ft. { Shales and grits with calcareous seams, underlain by epidotic grits and conglomerate.

To the north, in Raasay, the Diabaig Group is reduced in thickness to about 1,000 ft. Southwards of Skye, in Rum, a group of shales, 1,400 ft. thick, is regarded as corresponding to part of the Diabaig Group; and an overlying group of about 9,000 ft. of arkoses is believed to represent part at least of the Applecross grits.

In Skye the Torridonian strata are involved in the Caledonian thrust-movements. There, east of Loch Eishort, west of the Moine Thrust, the lower Diabaig Group is thrust over the Applecross grits, and these in turn over Cambrian quartzites, etc.; while farther north, south of Broadford, the grits are thrust on to Cambrian limestones. None of these movement-planes is considered to correspond to the Tarskavaig Thrust in the south of Sleat. In the complex Creag Strollamus area (south of Scalpay) contacts between Torridonian rocks and adjacent Cambrian limestones and Tertiary lavas have been interpreted in different ways (1953, 1954*a*, 1954*b*).

3. Moine Schists*: Ardnamurchan, Morvern and Mull
(*see* Fig. 6)

The Moine Thrust probably continues southwards from Skye to pass eastwards of the islands of Rum and Eigg, and is next located to the south-west of Mull, where it is considered to extend along the Sound of Iona. There the

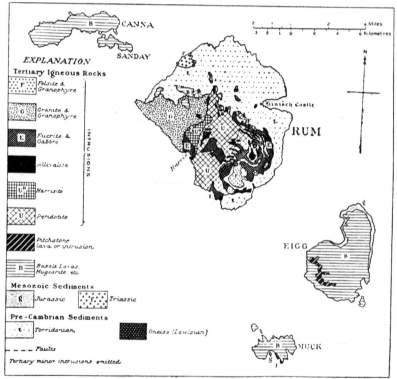

FIG. 5. *General Map of the Small Isles of Inverness-shire*
(Drawn from 1-in. Sheet 60, Geol. Surv., Scotland, with slight modification)

thrust serves to separate the Lewisian and supposed Torridonian rocks of Iona from the Moine Schists of the Ross peninsula. Southwards of Rum the thrust may have just touched the extreme western part of Ardnamurchan and from there crossed the north-west corner of Mull, but these areas are entirely covered by Mesozoic and Tertiary igneous rocks. Wherever the Tertiary basalt lavas and Mesozoic sediments have been removed by denudation in Ardnamurchan,

* For a description of the Tarskavaig Moine Schists of Sleat, *see* ' The Northern Highlands', British Regional Geology.

Morvern and Mull, the Moine Schists are encountered, except for local outcrops of Dalradian Schists, adjoining the Great Glen Fault in Mull, and of Lower Old Red Sandstone and Upper Carboniferous rocks.

In Ardnamurchan and Morvern the Moine Schists are extensively exposed, but in Mull, except for a few outcrops brought up in the centres of anticlines around the Tertiary plutonic masses, they are only found along the western coast south of Gribun and, farther south, in the Ross of Mull. In Ardnamurchan (1930) a somewhat lowly metamorphosed group of well-bedded schistose sandstones, or quartzose schists, with pebbly layers, often false-bedded, forms the main framework for the Tertiary intrusive masses. They are separated, along a line which may represent a major discordance, from more highly crystalline schists, which lie to the east. Farther south, these schists extend over Morvern eastwards from the Tertiary basaltic plateau. They consist of alternating belts of psammitic (quartzose) and garnetiferous pelitic (micaceous) schists with a prevalent north-south strike. Still farther east, pegmatitic injection becomes abundant, and many varieties of injection-gneisses are developed. Later igneous rocks include a great granitic mass belonging to the Caledonian suite which is composed of concentric belts of tonalite, granodiorite and granite, the latter forming the central member of the complex (1932). Minor intrusions are abundant and include sills of lamprophyre and diorite, etc. ('appinite' suite), earlier than the granite but cutting the injection-gneisses, and late dykes of porphyrite, quartz-dolerite, camptonite, monchiquite, olivine-dolerite, tholeiite, etc., ranging in age from Lower Old Red Sandstone to Tertiary.

In Western Mull especially in the Ross (1925) there are arkose granulites, often showing false-bedding. In the Ross there are in addition quartzites and pelitic schists with intrusive epidiorites (hornblende-schists). The pelitic schists contain streaks and lenticles of pegmatite, adjacent to which there are concentrations of tourmaline and kyanite crystals. The schists have been highly altered by the Ross of Mull granite with the development of sillimanite, andalusite and cordierite within a contact-aureole about a third of a mile wide (1949). The granite is pink or red in colour, and contains biotite together with a little muscovite. The brightly-hued rocky country formed of it is well known to everyone who has visited Iona.

4. DALRADIAN SCHISTS: MULL AND ARRAN (*see* Figs. 6, 7, 8)

In the east of Mull, at Loch Don (1925*b*), Dalradian Schists occur in the centre of an anticline, which is one of a series of concentric folds developed around an early mass of granophyre of the Tertiary Complex. The schists consist of grey slates and limestone, and the latter is correlated with the blue-grey limestone forming the island of Lismore near the mouth of Loch Linnhe. The Great Glen Fault, which extends along Loch Linnhe between Lismore and Morvern, must therefore have crossed Mull to the west of Loch Don, and in Mull the fault was probably bent southwards by the Tertiary folding movements. There is evidence that late displacements along it have affected the Mesozoic strata and Tertiary basalt lavas in Mull (Duart Bay, p. 36).

The schists of Arran are brought up in a great dome that almost completely surrounds the Tertiary granite in the northern half of the island. They consist mainly of grits and slates belonging to a lowly metamorphosed zone that lies along the southern margin of the Grampian Highlands. The cleavage or

B

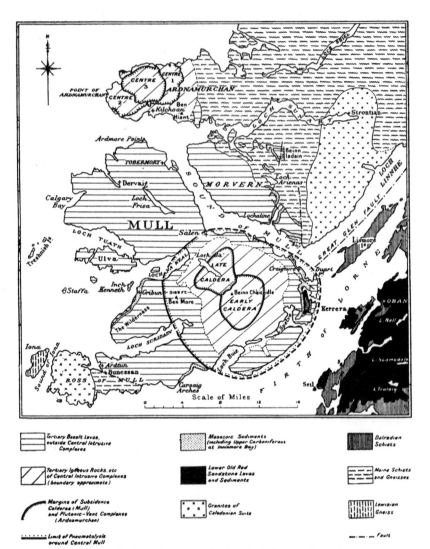

FIG. 6. *Sketch-map of the Mull–Ardnamurchan Area*
[Rep. from ' Guide to the Geological Model of Ardnamurchan ' (*Mem. Geol. Surv.*), 1934, Fig. 5]

schistosity is often well marked, and in the case of the finer-grained rocks may obscure the true bedding.

Partly on the evidence of graded bedding, the following succession has been inferred (1945a, 1947):

Quartzose grits, mainly of moderate to coarse grain . . III		
Dark shales with impersistent thin limestones		North
Pebbly quartzose grits		
Quartzo-feldspathic grits, mainly of moderate grain	II	Sannox
Fine grits and greenish slates		Grits
Quartzo-feldspathic grits mainly of moderate grain . . I		
Slates with subordinate grits . . . . Loch Ranza Slates		

The Loch Ranza Slates, which outcrop on both sides of the granite, are believed to occupy the core of an isoclinal fold, the limbs of which are formed by the North Sannox Grits. The slates are considered to be equivalent to the Aberfoyle Slates of the standard Dalradian Succession of Perthshire, and the North Sannox Grits I and II to the Leny/Ben Ledi Grits.

5. CAMBRIAN*: SKYE (see Fig. 4)

Strata of Cambrian age in Skye occur in two main outcrops, one to the south the other to the north of Loch Eishort (1910). The rocks have probably been thrust from the south-east by the great post-Cambrian movements, and were at one time largely covered by masses of Torridonian carried forward in turn along thrust-planes (p. 7). The thrusts have been folded into anticlines, in the centres of which the Cambrian rocks are exposed (1939).

A fairly complete succession is preserved in the area south of Loch Eishort, in Sleat. The beds overlie in their normal position the Torridonian grits and are also involved in complicated thrust-movements. Over a larger tract to the north of Loch Eishort and south-west of Broadford, practically only the uppermost beds of the Durness Limestone are found. These appear from beneath the over-thrust Torridonian rocks and form a curving anticline in the centre of which a Tertiary granite is intruded.

The succession is as follows:

		Estimated thicknesses ft.
DURNESS LIMESTONE	Dark limestone with fossils (Ben Suardal) and dark and white dolomite with cherts (Strath Suardal and Beinn an Dubhaich, and Sango-mhor beds)	—
	Flaggy and granular dolomite with chert in lumps and bands, with oolitic bands near base; including (in ascending order the Ghrudaidh, Eilean Dubh and Sailmhor beds ..	885
SERPULITE GRIT		50
FUCOID BEDS		60
QUARTZITE	Pipe-Rock (with vertical worm-tubes)	270
	False-bedded division	330

* According to modern knowledge the higher part of the Durness Limestone should be assigned to the Ordovician, see ' The Northern Highlands ', British Regional Geology.

The limestones and dolomites south-west of Broadford are in part altered to marble by the Tertiary intrusions, and have developed many metamorphic minerals (p. 92).

Olenellus and other fossils occur in the Fucoid Beds, and various annelids in the Pipe-Rock. In certain bands in the Ben Suardal limestones, fossils are abundant. From a limestone knoll about a mile and a half south of Broadford Hotel a dozen species of gastropods have been collected, together with several cephalopods, a lamellibranch and a sponge.

6. ORDOVICIAN: ARRAN (*see* Fig. 8)

In North Glen Sannox Arenig rocks form a narrow outcrop. On their west side they rest, without any apparent structural break, on Dalradian grits (1944); on their east side they are separated by faults partly from a narrow strip of Dalradian grits and partly from Lower Old Red Sandstone sediments.

The apparent succession is as follows:

	Estimated thicknesses ft.
' Upper ' greenstone (lava)	450
Black shale with chert and gritty or ashy bands	90
Brecciated lava	25
' Lower ' greenstone (lava)	375
Black shale	7
Brecciated lavaform rock	7
Black shale (resting on Dalradian grits)	26
TOTAL	980

The shales are much contorted in places while the cherts are granulitized. The lavas are basic in character and show well-marked ' pillow-structure '. The margins of the ' pillows ' are chilled and are bordered internally by zones of amygdales, characteristic features of the Arenig pillow-lavas of the South Ayrshire coast. A few thin sill-like intrusions are also present and include hornblende-gabbro, similar to gabbro associated with the Arenig lavas of South Ayrshire.

7. LOWER OLD RED SANDSTONE: MULL AND ARRAN
(*see* Figs. 6, 7, 8)

In the Loch Don Anticline in the south-east of Mull, a group of lavas intervenes between schists and Trias (1925b). They are greatly shattered, but there is little doubt that they form an extension of the Lower Old Red Sandstone lava group of the Lorne plateau around Oban, which consists chiefly of andesite.

In Arran, sediments of the same age are extensively exposed and locally include a volcanic horizon (1928). They enter into the great dome-structure surrounding the Northern Granite (1926a) and are also brought up in a smaller dome on the southern side of the Central Ring Complex. They are everywhere faulted against the schists. Lithologically they consist of coarse conglomerates, red mudstones and purplish or chocolate-coloured feldspathic sandstones. The

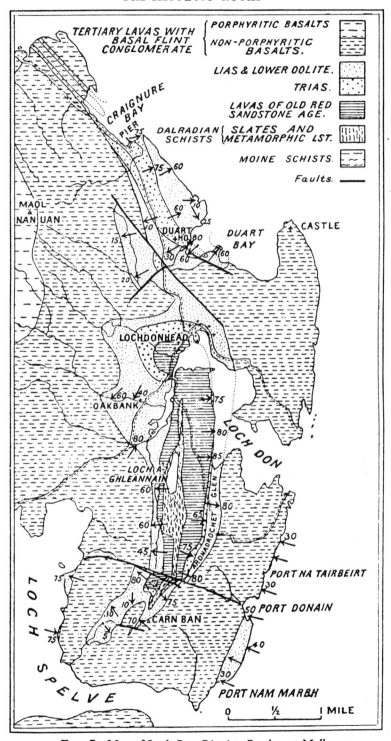

Fig. 7. *Map of Loch Don District, South-east Mull*
[Rep., with alterations, from ' Summary of Progress ' for 1909 *Mem. Geol. Surv.*), 1910, p. 28]

conglomerates contain blocks of quartzite, together with pebbles of andesite.

In Glen Shurig, south of the Northern Granite, plants have been collected at two horizons and belong to the Lower Old Red Sandstone genus *Psilophyton*. The volcanic horizon consists of a band of lava composed of hornblende-andesite and olivine-andesite. Overlying conglomerates to the south-east of Dougrie Point which contain lava-pebbles are apparently several thousands of feet thick.

8. Upper Old Red Sandstone: Arran (*see* Fig. 8)

The unconformity which in other areas separates the lower and upper divisions of the Old Red Sandstone cannot be recognized directly in Arran, owing to the absence of any marked difference in dip of the two series, though the unconformity no doubt exists. In the upper division the sandstones may be distinguished from those of the lower series by their brighter red colour and less feldspathic composition. When contact-altered, the beds of the lower division become grey in colour, and those of the upper division, which are more quartzose, turn white. The succession consists of alternations of sandstones, often false-bedded, with breccia-conglomerates made up of more or less angular fragments of quartz and schist. Mingled with these are well-rounded pebbles and blocks of quartzite derived from the conglomerates of the lower division (1928).

To the north of North Sannox a single basaltic lava-flow is intercalated in the sedimentary succession. Below the lava there are some 800 ft. of whitish conglomerates with pebbles of quartz and quartzite, together with flaggy sandstones. Above the lava come flaggy sandstones succeeded by higher conglomerates, associated with sandstone and cornstone in irregular bands.

A section on the northern coast east of Loch Ranza is famous in geological literature, for here James Hutton in 1795 demonstrated one of the great principles of geology (1795, 1802). On the shore, cornstone and sandstone are seen to rest unconformably upon the truncated ends of beds of schist. The two sets of strata are markedly discordant to one another and dip in opposite directions, the younger beds crossing the older, like the longer stroke of the Greek letter λ (1953*a*, 1954).

9. Lower Carboniferous: Arran (*see* Fig. 8)

As in other districts in Scotland, the Upper Old Red Sandstone in Arran passes upwards without any stratigraphical break into the Lower Carboniferous. The latter consists of two series, namely, the Calciferous Sandstone and Carboniferous Limestone (1928). The sequence is well displayed along the north-east coast near Laggan and Corrie, and again near Brodick Castle and in Glen Shurig. A great diminution in the thickness of all the divisions of the Carboniferous formation is evident as the beds are traced southwards. Total thicknesses, excluding volcanic rocks, are as follows:

	ft.
Laggan	2,275
Corrie	925
Brodick Castle and Glen Shurig	600

In the Calciferous Sandstone Series variously coloured sandstones are associated with red shales and cementstones, and there is a volcanic group consisting of basaltic lavas, tuffs and agglomerates. In the Carboniferous Limestone Series a lower group of limestones is separated from a higher calcareous group by a group of sandstones.

Near Laggan, a fossil bed containing typical Lower Carboniferous fish-remains and plants occurs at a low horizon in the Calciferous Sandstone Series. Higher up, in an alternating series of sandstones, cementstones and tuffs at the base of the volcanic succession, trees and plant-remains occur, together with a few lamellibranch shells. The fossil tree-trunks are embedded in ash and have their cellular structures perfectly preserved. The volcanic group, some 400 ft. in thickness, includes olivine-basalt lavas of the Dalmeny and Craiglockhart types well known in the Calciferous Sandstone lava-plateaus of the Midland Valley of Scotland.

At Corrie the volcanic group overlies cornstone-bearing strata assigned to the Upper Old Red Sandstone by E. B. Bailey (1926a). A main suite of lavas is succeeded by sediments (including a thin limestone) and a higher lava-flow a short distance below the Corrie Limestone which marks the base of the Carboniferous Limestone Series.

On the Laggan coast a sequence typical of the Carboniferous Limestone Series is found. The Corrie Limestone, which is correlated with the Hurlet Limestone of the Glasgow district, is succeeded by two calcareous bands corresponding to the well-known Hosie Limestones. These beds together with intervening strata thus represent the Lower Limestone Group of the Scottish Midland Valley. Overlying strata include at least one coal-seam, and represent the Limestone Coal Group. Succeeding marine horizons, of which there appear to be at least five, comprise the following:

Upper Limestone Group
5. Coral Limestone.
4. Cephalopod Limestone.
3. Limestone with abundant *Productus* (*Gigantoproductus*) *latissimus* J. Sowerby.
2. Fossiliferous ironstone.
1. Index Limestone.

At An Sgriob south of Corrie a sandstone of Upper Carboniferous age rests unconformably upon the Corrie Limestone, and higher portions of the Carboniferous Limestone Series are missing at this spot.

10. UPPER CARBONIFEROUS: ARRAN AND MORVERN
(*see* Figs. 6 and 8)

The Upper Carboniferous in Scotland includes the beds above the well-known palaeontological break, which occurs in the lower half of the Scottish Millstone Grit. None of the lower beds of the Millstone Grit has been identified in Arran, though they perhaps occur in an outcrop of the Millstone Grit on the Corrie shore. The sandstone unconformably overlying the Corrie Limestone at An Sgriob may belong to the upper part of the series (1928). In addition, a volcanic horizon underlying strata of Coal Measures age, exposed farther south in the head of the Sliddery Water, three miles west-south-west of Lamlash Bay, probably represents the Millstone Grit lavas of Ayrshire and their associated bauxitic clays. The general succession in this small outcrop of Upper Carboniferous beds is somewhat as follows:

5. Lavas, very slaggy, with occasional tuff-bands.
4. Coarse feldspathic grit.
3. Shales and ironstone bands.
2. Flaggy sandstones and shales, with fossils, passing westwards into fine volcanic mudstones.
1. Alternations of fine and coarse volcanic ash, etc., with beds apparently of lava.

Shales with an ironstone band, included with item 2 of the above succession, have yielded abundant ' mussels ' (*Anthracosia planitumida* Trueman and *Anthraconaia* aff. *aquilina* (J. de C. Sowerby)) that indicate the *similis-pulchra* Zone of the Coal Measures, together with plants and fish-remains. On the Corrie foreshore, Coal Measures mussels are again found, i.e. *Carbonicola oslancis* Wright, *C.* cf. *rhomboidalis* Hind, *Anthracosia* cf. *phrygiana* (Wright), *A.* cf. *regularis* (Trueman), *A. aquilina* (J. de C. Sowerby), *A. elliptica* (Wright) and *Naiadites triangularis* (J. de C. Sowerby), indicating the *modiolaris* Zone. It is very probable that the beds below this fossiliferous horizon belong to the *ovalis* Zone, but they are unfossiliferous. Near the Cock of Arran, *Naiadites* cf. *flexuosus* Trueman, a form typical of the *communis* and lower part of the *modiolaris* Zone, has been found (1942).

In Morvern, along Inninmore Bay on the Sound of Mull, Upper Carboniferous strata form the lower part of steep slopes capped by basalt lava cliffs (Fig. 6). Some 300 ft. of sandstones, often pebbly, together with occasional beds of shale and a thin seam of coal are present. The shales have yielded Carboniferous plants (1925b, 1934). The plants suggest that this northerly representation of the Carboniferous formation is of early Coal Measures age. No base is seen, but the beds no doubt rest directly upon the Moine Schists. Farther north, on Ben Hiant in Ardnamurchan, a few feet of sandstone, fireclay and sandy shales with obscure plants occur between schists and a basal Tertiary mudstone. These beds are perhaps to be correlated with the Carboniferous beds of Inninmore rather than grouped with the basal Tertiary sediments, to which they were tentatively assigned in the Ardnamurchan memoir.

11. PERMIAN: ARRAN (*see* Fig. 8)

The New Red Sandstone of Arran has been divided between the Permian and the Trias on lithological grounds (1915, 1928). The strata assigned to the Permian are estimated as 2,000 ft. in thickness, and their sequence is as follows:

4. Glen Dubh Sandstone
   White, yellow and pink, massive, calcareous sandstone.
3. Lamlash and Machrie Sandstones
   Coarse red sandstones, slightly false-bedded, sometimes thinly bedded.
2. Brodick Breccia
   Coarse quartz- and quartzitic-breccia with horizons rich in basalt and agate pebbles; thick lenticles of red dune-bedded sandstone.
1. Corrie Sandstone
   False-bedded brick-red sandstone with rounded wind-worn grains.

An unconformity at the base of the succession is most marked in the area around the southern and western sides of the Central Ring Complex. To the west, the Permian sandstones succeed the Upper Old Red Sandstone, and to the east, near the head of Benlister Glen, they rest directly upon the Corrie

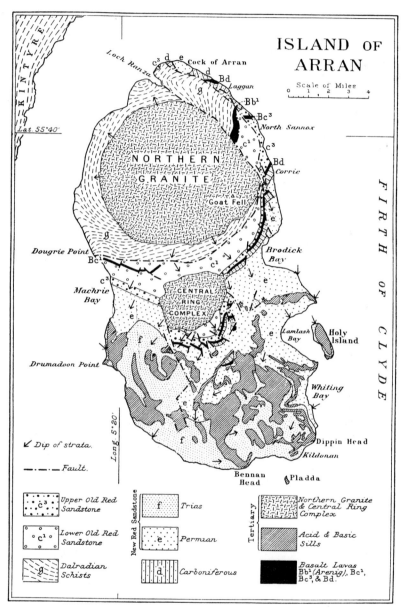

FIG. 8. *General Map of Arran*
(Based on Geological Survey maps)

Limestone at the base of the Carboniferous Limestone Series, while within a mile farther east they overlie the Coal Measures of the Sliddery Water. The denudation of the older Carboniferous rocks is demonstrated in the North of Arran by the occurrence of conglomerates containing pebbles of fossiliferous Carboniferous limestone near the base of the Permian sandstones.

Schist-fragments in the Brodick Breccia are biotite-bearing, and are more highly altered than the schists of Arran itself. Their source probably lay to the north or north-west in a more highly metamorphosed part of the South-west Highlands (1925a).

The desert climate that prevailed during the period is considered to be responsible for the reddening of the underlying Carboniferous rocks to considerable depths. Oxygen-bearing waters, percolating downwards, are believed to have altered the iron, which is present in the various kinds of beds in varying amounts, from the ferrous to the ferric state (1926).

REFERENCES

1795. J. HUTTON. *Theory of the Earth*. Edinburgh.
1802. J. PLAYFAIR. *Illustrations of the Huttonian Theory of the Earth*. Edinburgh.
1903. W. GUNN and others. The Geology of North Arran, etc. *Mem. Geol. Surv.*
1904. C. T. CLOUGH and A. HARKER. The Geology of West-Central Skye. *Mem. Geol. Surv.*
1908. A. HARKER. The Geology of the Small Isles of Inverness-shire. *Mem. Geol. Surv.*
1910. C. T. CLOUGH and others. The Geology of Glenelg, Lochalsh, and South-east Part of Skye. *Mem. Geol. Surv.*
1915. J. W. GREGORY. The Permian and Triassic Rocks of Arran. *Trans. Geol. Soc. Glasgow*, vol. xv, pt. ii, pp. 174–187.
1925. E. B. BAILEY and E. M. ANDERSON. The Geology of Staffa, Iona, and Western Mull. *Mem. Geol. Surv.*
1925a. B. H. BARRETT. The Permian Breccia of Arran. *Trans. Geol. Soc. Glasgow*, vol. xvii, pt. ii, pp. 264–270.
1925b. G. W. LEE and E. B. BAILEY. The Pre-Tertiary Geology of Mull, Loch Aline, and Oban. *Mem. Geol. Surv.*
1926. E. B. BAILEY. Subterranean Penetration by a Desert Climate. *Geol. Mag.*, vol. lxiii, pp. 276–280.
1926a. E. B. BAILEY. Domes in Scotland and South Africa: Arran and Vredefort. *Geol. Mag.*, vol. lxiii, pp. 481–495.
1928. G. W. TYRRELL. The Geology of Arran. *Mem. Geol. Surv.*
1930. J. E. RICHEY, H. H. THOMAS and others. The Geology of Ardnamurchan, North-west Mull and Coll. *Mem. Geol. Surv.*
1932. W. Q. KENNEDY and A. G. MACGREGOR. The Morvern–Strontian Granite. *In* Summary of Progress for 1931, Part II (*Mem. Geol. Surv.*), pp. 105–119.
1934. M. MACGREGOR and W. MANSON. The Carboniferous Rocks of Inninmore, Morvern. *In* Summary of Progress for 1933, Part II (*Mem. Geol. Surv.*), pp. 74–84.
1939. E. B. BAILEY. Caledonian Tectonics and Metamorphism in Skye. *Bull. Geol. Surv.*, No. 2, pp. 46–62.
1942. D. LEITCH. The Upper Carboniferous Rocks of Arran. *Trans. Geol. Soc. Glasgow*, vol. xx, pt. ii, pp. 141–154.
1944. J. G. C. ANDERSON and J. PRINGLE. The Arenig Rocks of Arran, and their Relationship to the Dalradian Series. *Geol. Mag.*, vol. lxxxi, pp. 81–87.
1944a. C. E. TILLEY. A Note on the Gneisses of Rhum. *Geol. Mag.*, vol. lxxxi, pp. 129–131.

1945. E. B. BAILEY. The Tertiary Igneous Tectonics of Rhum (Inner Hebrides). *Quart. Journ. Geol. Soc.*, vol. c for 1944, pp. 165–188.

1945a. J. G. C. ANDERSON. The Dalradian Rocks of Arran. *Trans. Geol. Soc. Glasgow*, vol. xx, pt. iii, pp. 264–286.

1946. W. Q. KENNEDY. The Great Glen Fault. *Quart. Journ. Geol. Soc.*, vol. cii, pp. 41–72.

1947. J. G. C. ANDERSON. The Geology of the Highland Border: Stonehaven to Arran. *Trans. Roy. Soc. Edin.*, vol. lxi, pt. ii, pp. 479–515.

1949. W. S. MacKENZIE. Kyanite–Gneiss within a Thermal Aureole. *Geol. Mag.*, vol. lxxxvi, pp. 251–254. (Ross of Mull).

1953. B. C. KING. Structure and Igneous Activity in the Creag Strollamus Area of Skye. *Trans. Roy. Soc. Edin.*, vol. lxii, pt. ii, pp. 257–402.

1953a. S. I. TOMKEIEFF. " Hutton's Unconformity", Isle of Arran. *Geol. Mag.*, vol. xc, pp. 404–408.

1954. J. G. C. ANDERSON. " Hutton's Unconformity ". *Geol. Mag.*, vol. xci, p. 85.

1954a. E. B. BAILEY. Relations of Torridonian to Durness Limestone in the Broadford–Strollamus District of Skye. *Geol. Mag.*, vol. xci, pp. 73–78.

1954b. E. B. BAILEY. Contact of Tertiary Lavas with Torridonian near Broadford, Skye. *Geol. Mag.*, vol. xci, pp. 105–115.

1955. E. B. BAILEY. Moine Tectonics and Metamorphism in Skye. *Trans. Edin. Geol. Soc.*, vol. xvi, pt. ii, pp. 93–166.

1960. J. SUTTON and J. WATSON. Sedimentary Structures in the Epidotic Grits of Skye. *Geol. Mag.*, vol. xcvii, pp. 106–122.

1960a. C. J. HUGHES. An occurrence of Tilleyite-bearing Limestones in the Isle of Rhum. *Geol. Mag.*, vol. xcvii, pp. 384–388.

1961. G. P. BLACK and W. WELSH. The Torridonian Succession of the Isle of Rhum. *Geol. Mag.*, vol. xcviii, pp. 265–276.

1961a. B. C. M. BUTLER. Metamorphism and metasomatism of rocks of the Moine Series by a Dolerite plug in Glenmore, Ardnamurchan. *Mineralogical Mag.*, vol. 32, pp. 866–897.

1963. R. C. SELLY, D. J. SHEARMAN, J. SUTTON and J. WATSON. Some Underwater Disturbances in the Torridonian of Skye and Raasay. *Geol. Mag.*, vol. 100, pp. 224–243.

III. MESOZOIC ROCKS

1. GENERAL SUCCESSION

IN THE INNER HEBRIDES stratified rocks of Mesozoic age outcrop around the margins of the Tertiary plateau basalt lavas, under cover of which they have been protected from erosion. They are to be seen mainly in two areas (Fig. 9): to the north, in the islands of Skye and Raasay; to the south, in the island of Mull and on the adjacent mainland of Morvern and Ardnamurchan. Certain divisions of the Jurassic and Cretaceous systems are exposed in the islands of Eigg and Muck. In Arran, only Triassic rocks are to be seen *in situ*, but Rhaetic, Liassic and Upper Cretaceous sediments have been preserved in a Tertiary volcanic vent.

The lithology is varied and includes sandstones, shales, limestones, seams of ironstone, lignite, oil-shale and jet. Certain lithological sequences extend over the whole region with little lateral variation and correspond fairly closely with the long-established divisions of the English sequence (Fig. 10). Faunal

STRATIGRAPHICAL SUBDIVISIONS		LITHOLOGICAL DESCRIPTION	MAXIMUM THICKNESS IN FEET
UPPER CRETA- CEOUS	Upper Chalk (Senonian) (Middle or Turonian Chalk absent) Greensand (Cenoman- ian)	Chalk with flints	12 (W. Mull)
		White sandstone with wind- rounded grains Greensand or calcareous grit	65 (Morvern)
LOWER CRETACEOUS AND UPPERMOST JURASSIC ABSENT			
UPPER JURASSIC	Kimmeridge Clay Corallian	Shales Calcareous grits, sandstones and shales, or blue shale	20+ (Skye) 180 (Skye)
	Oxford Clay Kellaways Beds	Shales Calcareous sandstone	100 (Skye) ? 25 (Skye)
MIDDLE JURASSIC	Cornbrash Great Estuarine Series Inferior Oolite	Gritty limestone Laminated shales with thin limestones and sandstone Limestone or calcareous sandstone, shales and sandstone	23 (Raasay) 600 (Skye) 600 (Raasay)
LOWER JURASSIC	Upper Lias Middle Lias (or Scalpa Sandstone) Lower Lias: Pabba Shales Broadford Beds Rhaetic	Shales with nodules and jet, and Raasay Ironstone White sandstone Sandy micaceous shales Limestones and shales Shales and sandy limestone	77 (Skye) 245 (Raasay) 700 (Skye) 340 (Raasay) 40 (W. Mull)

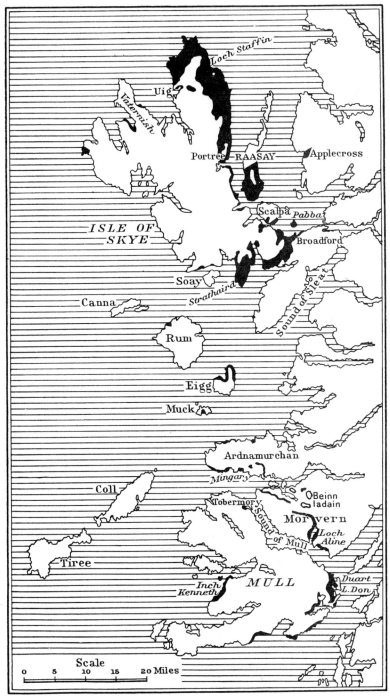

FIG. 9. *Map of the Inner Hebrides, showing Principal Outcrops of the Mesozoic Rocks (in black). Intrusions in Mesozoic Strata are omitted*

[Rep. with permission from ' A Synopsis of the Mesozoic Rocks of Scotland ', *Trans. Geol. Soc.*, Glasgow, vol. xix, part 1, 1932, Fig. 1 (slightly modified)]

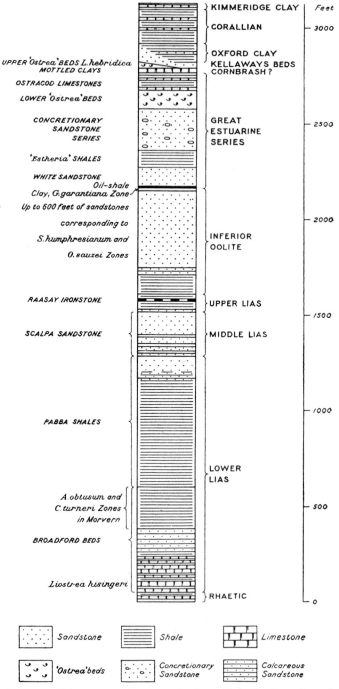

FIG. 10. *Sequence of the Jurassic Strata in the Inner Hebrides* (**mainly as developed in Skye and Raasay**)

For humphresianum read humphriesianum

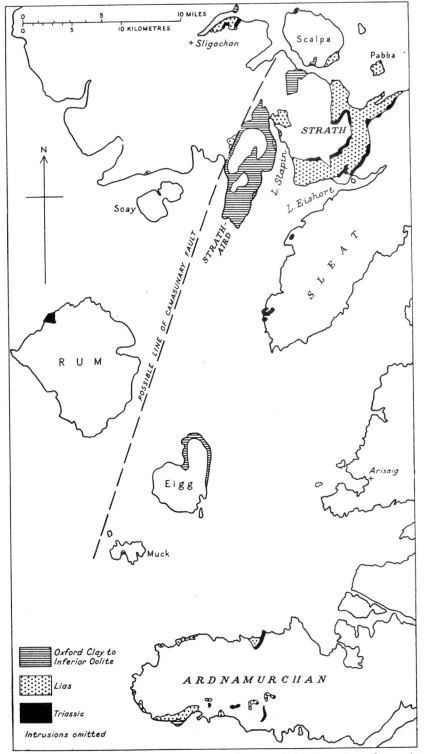

FIG. 11. *Sketch-map to illustrate the Distribution of the Jurassic and associated Triassic Rocks in the South of Skye–Ardnamurchan Area*

correlation in some detail with England and the Continent has been possible for parts of the succession, more particularly for the lower half of the Jurassic system in which ammonites are plentiful. (1878, 1932, 1933, 1934, 1934a and Survey Memoirs.)*

In the table on p. 20 the limits of each subdivision are based on the time-range of certain characteristic fossils, and do not necessarily correspond to horizons at which a lithological change takes place. So far as is known, the Jurassic sequence is incomplete in that only the very lowest beds of the Kimmeridge Clay are known. Higher horizons may be hidden beneath the Tertiary lavas of Skye or they may have been removed by erosion before the incursion of the Cretaceous sea.

In Morvern and over much of Mull, the Cretaceous Greensand rests upon Lower Lias, so that almost the whole of the Jurassic sediments have been removed. Faulting also took place during this period. One of the best known examples is found in Skye (Fig. 11) where, on the eastern side of the Camasunary Fault, beds up to and including Corallian are found, whereas on the western side all the higher Jurassic strata have been removed by erosion and the Tertiary lavas rest directly on the Lower Lias (Fig. 15).

The Cretaceous sequence is very incomplete. A greensand is fairly widely developed but its distribution suggests that the Cenomanian transgression took place over an irregularly eroded surface. These greensands are usually classified as Cenomanian which if correct means that the sea did not again reach the Hebridean area until Upper Cretaceous times. No representative of the Middle Chalk (Turonian) has been discovered and the Upper Chalk (Senonian) is at most (in Mull) 12 ft. thick.

The Tertiary was a period of igneous activity, of prolonged erosion and deep weathering. Erosion was even more active during the subsequent Glacial Period when the present topography was largely evolved. Since then there have been changes in sea level which left raised beaches, remnants of which can be detected at various levels.

2. TRIASSIC AND RHAETIC

(a) **Triassic.** Apart from crustacea, fish and plant-remains in the highest beds (probably Keuper) of Rum (1945), no fossils have been found in the Trias of the Western Highlands and the identification of the beds concerned is mainly dependent upon their stratigraphical position below and in conformity with the lowest Jurassic rocks, and upon their lithological similarity to the fossiliferous Trias of Elginshire. The character of the sediments indicates that freshwater and terrestrial conditions prevailed during the period.

In Arran a series of red marls, shales and sandstones, with sun-cracks and ripple-marks, upwards of 1,000 ft. in thickness, overlies the Permian breccias and desert sandstones, and has been correlated with the Keuper marls and Bunter sandstones of Dumfriesshire and the North of England (1915). The succession is as follows:

		Ft.
KEUPER	Levencorroch marls and cornstones, with calcareous sandstones, upwards of	260
	Auchenhew sandstones and shales	700
BUNTER	Lag a' Bheith marls and cornstones, with calcareous sandstones, thickness not known.	

* Dates within brackets refer to References on pp. 39-40.

In the Mull and Skye areas and in Rum Trias rests with marked unconformity on a variety of older rocks (Fig. 12). It varies much in thickness and was probably laid down upon a highly irregular floor. In Western Mull, for example, on the island of Inch Kenneth, the Trias is 200 ft. in thickness, but decreases southwards to only 10 ft. in a distance of two and a half miles. Beyond this point it again increases. In various sections, in the eastern parts of Mull and Ardnamurchan, and again in Central Skye, Lower Lias rests directly upon pre-Mesozoic rocks, and the Trias is entirely unrepresented.

The Hebridean Trias consists of massive conglomerates and breccias, corn-stones, red marls and sandstones, often calcareous. The conglomerates and breccias are composed of materials mainly derived from local rocks. In the southern area (Mull, Morvern, Ardnamurchan) the pebbles are chiefly of schist, together with vein-quartz, and, though the Trias locally rests upon Lower Old Red Sandstone lavas (Loch Don, p. 12) and Upper Carboniferous sand-stone (Inninmore Bay, p. 16), fragments of these rocks are sparse or absent. On the other hand, in conglomerates in Western Mull which rest upon Moine Schists, there are pebbles of Torridonian grits and Cambrian limestone which must have been transported for some miles from the west. In the Skye region to the north, where the Trias rests directly upon Torridonian grits and Cambrian quartzite and limestone, fragments of these rocks are abundant.

The cornstones occur in beds up to 20 ft. thick, or as nodules in the marls and sandstones. These chemically precipitated calcareous rocks are very similar to concretionary limestones forming at the present day in the superficial deposits of many tropical countries. The Hebridean cornstones are sometimes silicified, being traversed by interlacing veins of banded chert.

(b) **Rhaetic.** This series has been identified with certainty only in Western Mull, where some 40 ft. of beds of this age rest on the Trias (Fig. 12), in Arran, where its characteristic fossils have been collected from sediments faulted down into a vent of Tertiary age, and in Skye, where a few feet of sandy and calcareous strata containing badly preserved fossils possibly of Rhaetic age intervene between the Trias and the Lower Lias in several localities. The age of similar passage-beds found at one place in Raasay is less certain.

In Mull the Rhaetic consists of dark sandy limestones, and in Arran of black shales with thin limestones. The lamellibranchs *Pteria contorta* (Portlock), *Chlamys valoniensis* (Defrance) and *Protocardia rhaetica* (Merian) have been found in these beds so that they probably correspond to the lower part of the English sequence (*Pteria contorta* Zone); beds equivalent to the higher White Lias and Cotham Marble have not been found.

3. JURASSIC

This system consists of a lower marine series (Lias and Inferior Oolite) followed by estuarine deposits (Great Estuarine Series) after which marine conditions were again established (Oxford Clay, Corallian and Kimmeridge Clay). In the Lias and Inferior Oolite correlation with the English sequence by means of the ammonite faunas is reasonably complete. The Great Estuarine Series, however, though clearly the time equivalent of the Great Oolite, cannot be correlated in detail with that sub-division. Again, in the Oxford Clay, in the Corallian and in what now remains of the Kimmeridge Clay, the sequence of ammonite faunas is comparable with that found in Southern England.

(*a*) **Lias.** The lithological succession in the Lias is similar throughout the Hebridean region. Limestones and calcareous sandstones succeeded by sandy shales comprise the Lower Lias and are followed by Middle Lias sandstone capped by dark shales of Upper Lias age. In the Lower Lias the zonal sequence is as follows:

STAGES			ZONES	LOCALITY NUMBERS	SOME CHARACTERISTIC FOSSILS
PABBA SHALES	LOWER PLIENSBACHIAN OR CHARMOUTHIAN		*Prodactylioceras davoei*	?1, 5	*Androgynoceras maculatum* (Young & Bird)
			Tragophylloceras ibex	1, 4, 5	*Acanthopleuroceras valdani* (d'Orbigny)
			Uptonia jamesoni	1, 4, 5	*U. jamesoni* (J. de C. Sowerby), *U. bronni* (Roemer), *Epideroceras miles* (Simpson)
BROADFORD BEDS		SINEMURIAN	*Echioceras raricostatum* *Oxynoticeras oxynotum*	1, 4, 5 ?3	*Echioceras* (many species) *Gagaticeras?*
			Asteroceras obtusum	2, 3, 4	*Caenisites brooki* (J. Sowerby), *Xipheroceras aureum* (Young & Bird), *Promicroceras planicosta* (J. Sowerby)
			Caenisites turneri	?2, 5	*Caenisites turneri* (J. de C. Sowerby), *Microderoceras birchi* (J. Sowerby)
			Arnioceras semicostatum	1, 2, 3, 4, 5	*Euagassiceras sauzeanum* (d'Orbigny), *Paracoroniceras gmuendense* (Oppel), *Arnioceras* (many species)
			Arietites bucklandi	2, 5	*Metophioceras conybeari* (J. Sowerby)
		HETTANGIAN	*Schlotheimia angulata*	1, 3, 4, 6	*Calcirhynchia glevensis* (Davidson)
			Psiloceras planorbis	1, ?3, ?4	*P. planorbis* (J. de C. Sowerby), *P. sampsoni* (Portlock)
			pre-*planorbis* Beds	1, 5	*Liostrea hisingeri* (Nilsson)

Localities: 1, Mull; 2, Morvern; 3, Ardnamurchan; 4, Skye; 5, Raasay; 6, Arran.

The lower part of the Broadford Beds (Hettangian Stage) contains few ammonites, but is rich in a shallow-water fauna, including oysters, gastropods and corals. Shelly limestones largely composed of *Liostrea hisingeri* (Nilsson) are locally present. The remaining part of the Broadford Beds (Sinemurian Stage) is well developed in the Hebridean region. The Broadford Beds are more

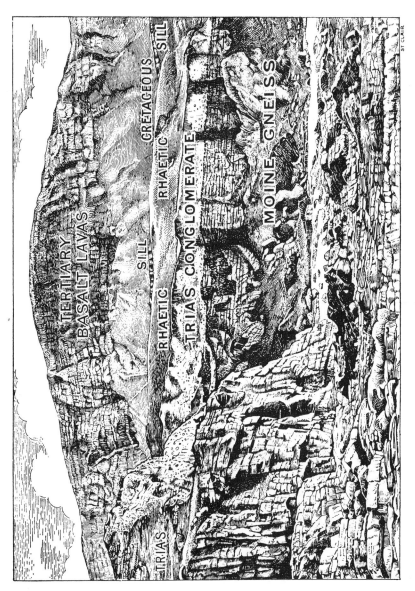

FIG. 12. *View showing Pre-Tertiary Strata and Tertiary Plateau Lavas near Gribun, W. Mull* [Rep. from 'The Geology of Staffa, Iona, and Western Mull' (*Mem. Geol. Surv.*), 1925, Fig. 6]

shaly and thicker in Skye than further south where, in Ardnamurchan, Morvern and Mull, limestone is strongly developed. The sequence up to and including the *A. semicostatum* Zone (i.e. the top of the thick limestones of the Mull area), consists of about 340 ft. of beds in Raasay, 240 ft. in Skye and only about 100 ft. in Morvern and Ardnamurchan. The overlying shaly beds in Morvern, however, representing the *C. turneri* and *A. obtusum* Zones are 182 ft. in thickness. Of these beds, the upper 160 ft. belong to the *A. obtusum* Zone, which is represented by only a few feet of shales south of Broadford and which has not been recognized in Raasay.

It should be noted that the beds corresponding to the *C. turneri* and *A. obtusum* Zones have been grouped with the Pabba Shales in the memoir dealing with the pre-Tertiary rocks of Mull and the Loch Aline district of Morvern; but that in the Ardnamurchan memoir the original upper limit for the Broadford Beds proposed by H. B. Woodward in Skye was reverted to.

The general sequence of the Broadford Beds in Skye is as follows:

		Ft.
SINEMURIAN STAGE	Shaly beds, including earthy limestones representing the *A. bucklandi* and *A. semicostatum* Zones	125
	Sandstones, with quartz-conglomerate and sandy limestone	25
HETTANGIAN STAGE	Limestones, with bands of quartz-conglomerate, with a bed of corals (*Thecosmilia martini* (Fromentel) and *Liostrea*, etc.)	65–75
	Sandstones and limestones, with quartz-conglomerate ..	10–15

The shales which occur at the top of the Broadford Beds, as defined by Woodward, are similar lithologically to the overlying micaceous sandy shales that are characteristic of the Pabba Shales. The latter reach a maximum thickness. of 600–700 ft. in Skye and Raasay, and decrease southwards to about 400 ft. in Mull. Both in Mull and Skye these beds have yielded many fossils and extensive lists are published in the Geological Survey Memoirs. In Raasay these beds contain a rich fauna and in the *E. raricostatum* Zone, which is over 350 ft. thick, ammonites are especially abundant. The sediments are dark sandy shales with clay ironstone and foetid limestone nodules, but become more and more sandy towards the top, where shaly sandstones are developed.

The *Middle Lias* (*Scalpa Sandstone*) is composed of sandstone, usually white, and often massive, forming steep cliffs and bold escarpments. Fossils are specially plentiful in calcareous doggers in the sandstone. Ammonites are rare, but the brachiopods and lamellibranchs allow of a comparison with the English sequence. Shallow-water forms, such as *Gryphaea, Pseudopecten, Plicatula*, etc., are chiefly met with. The zonal sequence is as follows:

STAGE	ZONES	LOCALITY NUMBERS	SOME CHARACTERISTIC FOSSILS
SCALPA SANDSTONE — UPPER PLIENSBACHIAN OR DOMERIAN	*Pleuroceras spinatum*	?1, 2, 3, 4	*P. spinatum* (Bruguière), *Tetrarhynchia tetrahedra* (J. Sowerby)
	Amaltheus margaritatus	1, 3, 4	*A. margaritatus* (Montfort), *A. stokesi* (J. Sowerby), *Amauroceras ferrugineum* (Simpson)

Localities: 1, Mull; 2, Skye; 3, Scalpa; 4, Raasay.

In Raasay, east of Dun Caan (Fig. 13), the Middle Lias reaches its thickest development, and the following succession is exposed:

		Ft.
	Muddy sandstone with *Dactylioceras* (Upper Lias) ..	12
	Calcareous sandstone	2
	Muddy sandstone with doggers and a band of *Pseudo-*	
DOMERIAN	*pecten aequivalvis* (J. Sowerby)	111
STAGE	Alternation of sandstone and sandy shales with a band	
(MIDDLE LIAS)	of *Gryphaea gigantea* (J. de C. Sowerby) 30 ft. from	
	top (towards base of *P. spinatum* Zone)	100
	Sandstone with carbonaceous markings, with *Gryphaea*	
	cymbium Schäfle and *Pseudopecten aequivalvis* ..	20

Ammonites are not sufficiently abundant to make possible an exact determination of the limits for the two zones represented but it would appear that the uppermost 150 ft. of strata, or thereabouts, belong to the *P. spinatum* Zone and the underlying 90 ft. or so to the *A. margaritatus* Zone.

In Skye the Middle Lias is probably similar in thickness to that in Raasay but in the area south of Portree the ground is faulted and slipped and often difficult of access and further south near Holm only the upper part is exposed. The top is here a crinoidal limestone with nests of Rhynchonellids.

The Upper Lias is very like that of England, both faunally and lithologically. As in Yorkshire and Dorset the strata consist of dark micaceous shales with argillaceous nodules, pyrites and jet. The zonal sequence is as follows:

STAGE	ZONES	LOCALITY NUMBERS	SOME CHARACTERISTIC FOSSILS
TOARCIAN	*Lytoceras jurense*	2, 3, 4	*Pleydellia aalensis* (Zieten), *P. costulatum* (Zieten), *Grammoceras sp.*, *Alocolytoceras sp.*
	Hildoceras bifrons	1, 4	*H. bifrons* (Bruguière), *Dactylioceras commune* (J. Sowerby), *Peronoceras attenuatum* (Simpson)
	Harpoceras falcifer	1, 2, 3, 4	*H. falcifer* (J. Sowerby), *H. exaratum* (Young & Bird), *H. mulgravium* (Young & Bird), *Eleganticeras elegantulum* (Simpson), *Inoceramus dubius* J. de C. Sowerby
	Dactylioceras tenuicostatum	3, 4, 5	*Dactylioceras spp.*

Localities: 1, Mull; 2, Ardnamurchan; 3, Skye; 4, Raasay; 5, Shiant Isles.

Rocks of Upper Lias age are exposed in various sections from the southern coast of Mull to the Shiant Isles north of Skye. The group is everywhere thin, except in the area north of Portree in Skye where the thickness is not less than 100 ft.

Ft.

Sandstone (base of Inferior Oolite) 50

UPPER LIAS
{
Shaly sandstone (? *L. jurense* Zone) 25
Oolitic ferruginous limestone (= Raasay Ironstone) .. .. up to 5¾
Micaceous shales with thin limestone bands and nodules (*H. falcifer*
   Zone and ? *H. bifrons* Zone) .. .. about 55
Jet band 0–1
Micaceous shales (? *D. tenuicostatum* Zone) .. .. .. about 14
}

In Raasay the ironstone is 8 ft. thick, and was at one time intensively worked (p. 117). It is an oolitic limy ironstone in which the iron is present largely in the form of the green silicate, chamosite, as in the Cleveland Ironstone of Yorkshire which occurs, however, at a lower stratigraphical level. The Raasay ironstone accumulated slowly on the sea floor and consequently is often very fossiliferous indeed.

(*b*) **Inferior Oolite.** This series is well developed in the Hebridean region and the faunal sequence is remarkably similar to that of England.

The zonal sequence is as follows:

STAGE	ZONES	LOCALITY NUMBERS	SOME CHARACTERISTIC FOSSILS
BAJOCIAN	*Parkinsonia parkinsoni** *Garantiana garantiana*	1, 3, 4	*G.* cf. *garantiana* (d'Orbigny), *G. coronata* Wetzel
	Strenoceras subfurcatum	4	*S. subfurcatum* (Zieten)
	Stephanoceras humphriesianum	1, 3, 4	*S. humphriesianum* (J. Sowerby), *Teloceras* cf. *coronatum* (Quenstedt)
	Otoites sauzei	1, 3	*Sonninia alsatica* (Haug), *S.* (*Papilliceras*) *mesacantha* (Waagen), *Poecilomorphus macer* S. Buckman
	Sonninia sowerbyi	1, 2, ? 3, 4	*Darellia polita* S. Buckman, *Graphoceras elegantulum* (S. Buckman)
	Ludwigia murchisonae	1, 2, 3, 4	*L. murchisonae* (J. de C. Sowerby), *Graphoceras concavum* (J. Sowerby), *G. magnum* (S. Buckman), *Pseudoglossothyris simplex* (J. Buckman)
	Tmetoceras scissum	1, 2, 3, 4	*Tmetoceras reglyi* (Dumortier), *Leioceras thomsoni* S. Buckman, *L. plicatellum* S. Buckman
	Leioceras opalinum	1, 3, 4	*Leioceras opaliniforme* (S. Buckman)

Localities: 1, Mull; 2, Ardnamurchan; 3, Skye; 4, Raasay.

* Not represented by marine strata.

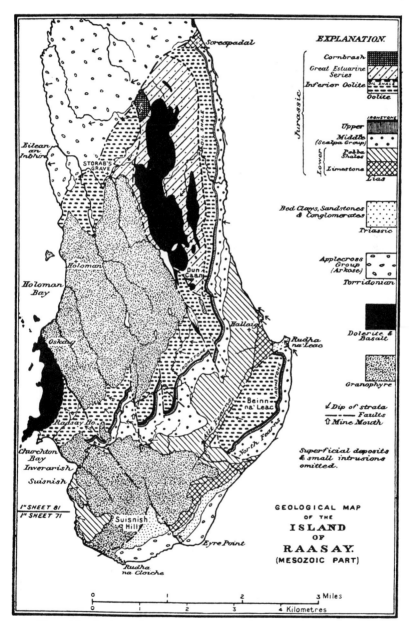

FIG. 13. *Geological Map of the Island of Raasay* (*Mesozoic part*)
[Rep. from ' The Iron Ores of Scotland ' (*Mem. Geol. Surv.*), 1920, Fig. 16 (slightly modified)]

The Inferior Oolite is thickest in Skye and Raasay (up to 600 ft. in Raasay, 375 ft. in Skye) and becomes thinner and more calcareous in Ardnamurchan (120 ft.) and Mull (95 ft.). The thinness of the lower half of the series in Mull is remarkable; in the Ardnadrochet Glen for example the three zones *L. opalinum*, *T. scissum* and *L. murchisonae* are represented by only 6 ft. of sandy limestone. In North-eastern Skye the ammonites are very well preserved, particularly in the *L. murchisonae* and *O. sauzei* Zones. The highest zone to be recognized is represented by a dark clay containing the ammonite *Garantiana garantiana* (d'Orbigny) and is found in Skye, Raasay and Mull. This is succeeded by a bituminous horizon which may be an oil-shale, a black sandstone or an impure coal and which marks the base of the Great Estuarine Series.

The lithological sequence exposed along the cliffs of North-east Skye is typical of the northern area:

		Ft.
	Oil-shale horizon (Great Estuarine Series)	—
INFERIOR OOLITE	*Garantiana* clay	5
	Calcareous grit	20
	Yellow sandstone with calcareous bands and doggers ..	150
	Blue-grey shaly sandstone	150
	Yellow sandstone	50
	Shaly sandstone (Upper Lias)	—

In Raasay the main mass of sandstone is 600 ft. thick as compared with the 370 ft. in Skye. At the base the ammonite zones from *T. scissum* to *S. sowerbyi* are represented in a small thickness of sediment (Pl. II). Thus the greater part of this thick sandstone probably corresponds only to the *O. sauzei* and *S. humphriesianum* Zones, since, as in Skye, it is overlain by a bed of clay which represents the *S. subfurcatum* and *G. garantiana* Zones.

In Ardnamurchan and Mull limestones become more prominent, but west of Kilchoan in Ardnamurchan there is again a thick sandstone at the horizon of the Raasay sandstone (Fig. 14). The sequence is as follows, the thicknesses given being somewhat approximate:

		Ft.
	Barren sandstone, partly reddish (? *O. sauzei* and *S. humphriesianum* Zones)	60
S. sowerbyi,	Shaly flags	15
L. murchisonae &	Limestone with bands of shale	25
T. scissum Zones	Calcareous sandstone	15

(*c*) **Great Estuarine Series.** The Inferior Oolite is followed without any apparent break by a great thickness of beds of estuarine character and fauna. At the top they pass into strata apparently of Cornbrash age thus corresponding to the Bathonian and the greater part of the Vesulian of Southern England; and approximately, to the Upper Estuarine Beds of Yorkshire. In the absence of marine fossils, particularly ammonites, more detailed correlation is not possible (*see* tabular statement on p. 34).

The series is widely distributed, being well developed on the east coast of Scotland (Brora) as well as throughout the Hebridean area from Raasay and Skye southwards to Ardnamurchan and probably to Mull. In North Skye it attains its maximum thickness of about 600 ft., over 400 ft. in South-east Skye (Strathaird), over 300 ft. in Eigg, but in Ardnamurchan (and possibly Mull) only small remnants have escaped denudation.

The thickest and most complete sequence in the Great Estuarine Series is that seen in the north of Skye. The following sub-divisions have been proposed:

Ft.

8. Upper ' Ostrea' Beds—shales with *Liostrea hebridica* 35
7. Mottled Clays—marly, red and green mottled clays with thin sandstone
   ribs—no fossils other than plant debris 43
6. Ostracod Limestones—shales and thin limestones with ' *Estheria* ',
   ostracods, ' *Cyrena* ' etc. 90
5. Lower ' Ostrea ' Beds—dark shales etc. with *Liostrea hebridica* in great
   abundance 60–120
4. Concretionary Sandstone Series—soft yellow sandstone with calcareous
   ribs and doggers 220
3. ' *Estheria* ' shales—dark fissile shales and thin impure limestones with
   ' *Estheria* ', ostracods, fish etc. 90
2. White Sandstone—massive unfossiliferous white sandstone 30–100
1. Oil Shale, sometimes a poor coal, passing into a black sandstone
   laterally 7–10

At least two of the thin limestones in the ' Estheria ' shales are algal and
there is an algal band about 4 in. thick in the Lower Ostrea Beds which has been
traced over a wide area (1948a). In South-east Skye, nearer the centre of the
sedimentary basin, there is less coarse sediment and the Concretionary Sandstone Series is represented by only 70 ft. or so of sandy limestones and shales.
Similarly in Raasay, the thickness of the series is only about half that of North
Skye. Further south, in Eigg, towards the southern margin of the basin, the
calcareous sandstones are 200 ft. thick. In Muck they are only 30 ft. in thickness.

In Ardnamurchan only the ' Estheria ' shale division has been recognized,
here about 8 ft. thick.

The Lower Ostrea Beds group is a muddy shell bank full of *Liostrea hebridica*
and was one of the earliest sub-divisions to be recognized. It is found in
Skye, Raasay, Eigg and Muck. In Raasay sandy limestones which appear
to be the equivalent of the Mottled Clay division of Skye contain fossils which
include *Cererithyris intermedia* (J. Sowerby) and indicate a position in the
Lower Cornbrash. The Upper Ostrea Beds are only seen in North Skye and may
represent an impersistent shell bank belonging to the underlying Mottled Clays
or the overlying Belemnite Sands.

(*d*) Kellaways Beds. In North Skye the marine Oxford Clay is separated from
the estuarine beds below by some 25 ft. of soft argillaceous sand near the middle
of which is a 2-ft. hard calcareous, very fossiliferous sandstone. The fauna
consists largely of marine lamellibranchs suggesting equivalence with the
Kellaways Beds of England, but in the absence of identifiable ammonites this
correlation is not certain. In South Skye the Mottled Clays are followed by a
dark, coarse sandstone with casts of belemnites and pockets of brachiopods
etc., which include *Ornithella kellawaysensis*. This stratum in Strathaird and the
Belemnite Sands of North Skye appear to be the equivalent of the Brora Roof
Bed on the east coast of Scotland, which is a 6-ft. calcareous sandstone.

In Eigg also the uppermost beds of the Great Estuarine Series are succeeded
by a calcareous sandstone at the base of which is a Belemnite–Lamellibranch
fauna resembling that of the Belemnite Sands of North Skye.

(*e*) Oxford Clay. The only satisfactory section of the Oxford Clay is to be
found in Staffin Bay, on the north-east coast of Skye. Here a series of dark
shales with thin grey cementstones, though badly faulted, has yielded ammonites
indicating the presence of all the zones from *K. jason* to *C. cordatum*. Corallian
shales succeed without any change of facies and can only be distinguished from
the Oxford Clay below by their fauna.

GREAT ESTUARINE SERIES IN THE INNER HEBRIDES

	N. SKYE[1]	S.E. SKYE[2]	RAASAY[3]	EIGG[4]	MUCK[4]	DORSET[5]
KELLAWAYS BEDS	Belemnite Sands 25 ft.	Black sandstone	not exposed	Calcareous Sandstone 12 ft.		Kellaways Clay 80 ft.
	Upper 'Ostrea' Beds 35 ft.	missing	not exposed or missing?	?		— ? —
	Mottled Clays and sandstone 43 ft.	Blue shaly marl 40 ft.	Sandy limestone 23 ft.	?		Cornbrash 30 ft.
	Ostracod Limestones 90 ft.	'Paludina' scotica Limestone and shales 77 ft.	not exposed	Ostracod Shales and limestones 21 ft.	Cementstone Group 20 ft.	— ? —
	Lower 'Ostrea' Beds 120 ft.	'Ostrea' hebridica Beds 17 ft.	'Ostrea' hebridica Beds	'Ostrea' hebridica Shales 31 ft.	'Ostrea' hebridica Group 65 ft.	Forest Marble 80 ft.
GREAT ESTUARINE SERIES	Concretionary Sandstone Series 220 ft.	'Cyrena' Limestones 70 ft.	Calcareous Sandstone	'Cyrena' Limestone 20 ft.	Calcareous Sandstone Group 30 ft.	— ? —
			} 250 ft.	Calcareous Sandstone 200 ft.		
	'Estheria' Shales 90 ft.	'Cyrena' Shales 200 ft.	'Cyrena' Shales and sandstones	Lower Shales 45 ft.		Fuller's Earth 150 ft.
	White Sandstone 100 ft.	White Sandstone 40 ft.	Sandstone			— ? —
	Oil-shale, coal or black sandstone 10 ft.	Grey micaceous shaly flags 20 ft.	Oil-shale 10 ft.	?		
INFERIOR OOLITE	G. garantiana Clay 10 ft.	Black shale with G. garantiana 10 ft.	G. garantiana Clay 10 ft.			Upper Inferior Oolite

[1] F. W. Anderson 1948   [2] Based on C. B. Wedd 1910   [3] Based on G. W. Lee 1920   [4] Based on G. Barrow 1908   [5] Based on A. M. Davies 1929

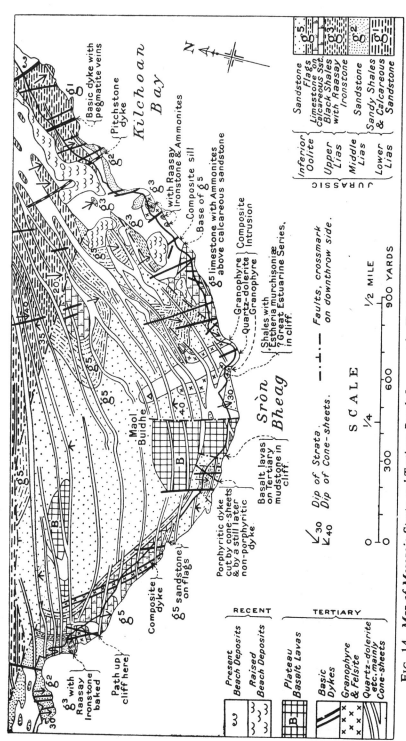

FIG. 14. *Map of Mesozoic Strata and Tertiary Basalt Lavas cut by Tertiary Minor Intrusions, West of Kilchoan Bay*

NOTE—Tertiary cone-sheets are mainly represented diagrammatically.
[Rep. from ' The Geology of Ardnamurchan', etc. (*Mem. Geol. Surv.*), 1930, Fig. 3]

In the south of Skye the Oxford Clay is largely represented by dark, shaly, micaceous and calcareous sandstones with some shaly beds. Ammonites are present but very poorly preserved and it is not until near the top where the more argillaceous beds begin to predominate that recognizable forms are found which indicate the *C. cordatum* Zone. Here the whole of the Oxford Clay is probably represented by about 80 ft. of sandy strata as compared with the 100 ft. of shales forming this group in North Skye.

In Eigg the greater part of the Oxford Clay may be represented by a bed of limestone some 8 ft. thick and perhaps by part of the underlying sandstone. The limestone is succeeded by soft friable dark-grey shales which contain *C. cordatum* and so may represent the uppermost Oxford Clay and probably the basal Corallian.

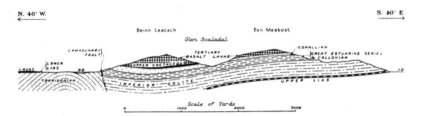

FIG. 15. *Section across the Strathaird Peninsula, Skye*

[Redrawn from Fig. 3, ' The Geology of Glenelg, Lochalsh and South-east Part of Skye ' (*Mem. Geol. Surv.*), 1910]

(*f*) **Corallian.** This series is well developed in North Skye, where about 180 ft. of shales with thin cementstones like those of the Oxford Clay below have yielded ammonites which indicate that the whole of the Corallian is represented. The uppermost 40 ft. contains *Pictonia baylei* which suggests that the lowest beds of the Kimmeridge Clay are also present.

In South-east Skye the lowest ammonite fauna so far recorded is that at the junction of the Oxford Clay and Corallian. Above are some 200 ft. of shaly beds with a fauna mainly of Perisphinctids representing a higher horizon in the Corallian. No trace of uppermost Corallian or Kimmeridge Clays has been found. In Eigg again only the lowest beds of the Corallian have been identified. There are no extensive exposures and the thickness of Corallian shales is unknown.

(*g*) **Kimmeridge Clay.** Unlike the extensive development of this series on the east coast of Scotland, in the Hebridean region only fragments remain. Following on the Corallian Shales in Staffin Bay and in an inlier east of Uig, both in North Skye, are dark shales and cementstones with ammonites which suggest that some at least of the lowest Kimmeridge Clay is present. But it is almost certain that higher beds lie hidden beneath the Tertiary lavas in the ground between these two localities.

In South-eastern Mull, from baked shales exposed in a stream that flows into Duart Bay, ammonites allied to the genus *Rasenia* indicate an early Kimmeridge Clay age. It is thought that the strata concerned have fallen down a fault fissure and that the fault is a continuation of the Great Glen Fault, along a branch of which movement in Kimmeridge Clay times is supposed to have taken place near Helmsdale on the Sutherland coast.

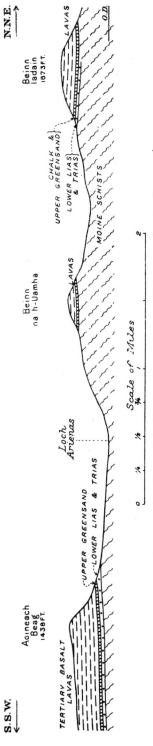

FIG. 16. *Section across Part of the Tertiary Lava-plateau of Morvern. showing Lava-outliers*

4. UPPER CRETACEOUS

In the Hebridean region widespread if thin deposits of Upper Cretaceous age rest unconformably on a denuded surface composed of Jurassic, Triassic and older rocks. The extent of this intra-Mesozoic erosion has been already indicated, and also the fact that the Upper Cretaceous was curtailed by denudation in its turn after the deposition of the Chalk and before the outbreak of volcanic activity in early Tertiary times (p. 24).

The succession typical of Mull and Morvern attains a maximum thickness on Beinn Iadain, beneath an outlier of the Tertiary basalt lavas of the Morvern plateau (Fig. 16), and is as follows:

		Ft.	In.
TERTIARY	{ Basalt lavas	—	—
	{ Sediments	1	5
UPPER CHALK (Senonian)	Chalk, silicified, with numerous flint nodules, with *Salenia* cf. *geometrica* Agassiz etc. ..	1	2
	Turonian apparently absent		
GREENSAND (Cenomanian)	Brownish clay, with small terebratulid and rhynconellid brachiopods, *Gryphaeostrea canaliculata* (J. Sowerby), *Neithea sexcostata* (Woodward) and *Cinulia avellana* (Brongniart)	—	11
	White quartzose sandstone, with wind-rounded grains	24	—
	Glauconitic calcareous sandstone with two bands of sandy limestone with *Exogyra conica* (J. Sowerby), *Gervillella sublanceolata* (d'Orbigny), numerous pectinids and a large nautiloid; above a band of grit with quartz pebbles resting on greensand	40	9
LOWER LIAS	Brownish clay and limestone	3	8

The occurrence of the echinoderm *Salenia* cf. *geometrica* confirms the conclusion reached by J. W. Judd that the Chalk of Morvern belongs to the Senonian (1934a). The zonal fossil *Belemnitella mucronata* was recorded by Judd, indicating a high level in the Senonian (1878), but no further examples have been obtained.

At Lochaline village on the coast of Morvern the White Sandstone is 40 ft. in thickness, and is an almost pure silica rock. At Gribun, in Western Mull, a similar sequence is again exposed. Greensand with *Exogyra conica* (J. Sowerby) and *Aequipecten asper* (Lamarck), unconformably overlying the Rhaetic and Lower Lias, is succeeded by the White Sandstone, 12 ft. thick, followed by 12 ft. of silicified Chalk. The Chalk is penetrated by fissures filled with wind-rounded quartz-grains, indicating a continuation of desert conditions after the upheaval of the Chalk.

E. B. Bailey has drawn interesting conclusions concerning the physiography of the Upper Cretaceous period from the occurrence of the wind-rounded sands of Morvern and Mull and from the fact that rounded sand grains are sporadically found in the Chalk of England and France (1924). A mature desert, he considers, fringed the northern shores of the relatively shallow Chalk sea. No rivers crossed the belt of desert, and the freedom of the chalky oozes from terrigenous materials is thus explained.

In South-eastern Mull (Loch Don) greensand, 10 ft. thick, is exposed beneath a Tertiary pebble-bed of flints, and contains, among other fossils, *Schloenbachia intermedia* (Mantell). This ammonite definitely fixes the Cenomanian age of the deposits.

In Eigg, Upper Cretaceous sandstone and glauconitic marl overlie the Lower Corallian. In the northern area the sequence is somewhat similar to that found in Mull and Morvern. Near Allt Stroilamus on the east coast of Skye a limestone, 15 ft. in thickness, contains fragments of *Inoceramus* and many species of foraminifera, and is considered to be altered Chalk. An underlying calcareous grit with *Exogyra* cf. *conica* and other fossils, exposed in the adjoining island of Scalpa, is correlated with the Greensand.

In addition to the scattered remnants of Chalk found beneath the Tertiary basalt lavas of the west of Scotland, the chances of denudation have exposed considerable masses that have slipped down into a Tertiary vent in the island of Arran (p. 108). From some of these, fossils typical of the Chalk have been obtained.

REFERENCES

1873. J. Bryce. On the Jurassic Rocks of Skye and Raasay. *Quart. Journ. Geol. Soc.*, vol. xxix, pp. 317–351.

1878. J. W. Judd. The Secondary Rocks of Scotland. Third Paper. The Strata of the Western Coast and Islands. *Quart. Journ. Geol. Soc.*, vol. xxxiv, pp. 660–741.

1908. G. Barrow. *In* The Geology of the Small Isles of Inverness-shire. *Mem. Geol. Surv.* (pp. 20, 23–26).

1910. C. B. Wedd. *In* The Geology of Glenelg, Lochalsh and South-east Part of Skye. *Mem. Geol. Surv.* (pp. 116, 121).

1915. J. W. Gregory. The Permian and Triassic Rocks of Arran. *Trans. Geol. Soc. Glasgow*, vol. xv, pt. ii, pp. 174–187.

1920. G. W. Lee. *In* The Mesozoic Rocks of Applecross, Raasay and North-east Skye. *Mem. Geol. Surv.* (pl. viii).

1924. E. B. Bailey. The Desert Shores of the Chalk Seas. *Geol. Mag.*, vol. lxi, pp. 102–116.

1929. A. M. Davies. In *Handbook of the Geology of Great Britain*. London (p. 378c).

1932. G. W. Lee and J. Pringle. A Synopsis of the Mesozoic Rocks of Scotland. *Trans. Geol. Soc. Glasgow*, vol. xix, pt. i, pp. 158–224.

1933. W. J. Arkell. *The Jurassic System in Great Britain*. Oxford.

1933a. J. E. Richey. Summary of the Geology of Ardnamurchan. *Proc. Geol. Assoc.*, vol. xliv, pt. I, pp. 1–56. (Excursion Guide.)

1933b. L. F. Spath. The Invertebrate Faunas of the Bathonian–Callovian Deposits of Jameson Land (East Greenland). *Meddelelser om Grönland*. Copenhagen, 1932, p. 149.

1934. Malcolm MacGregor. The Sedimentary Rocks of North Trotternish, Isle of Skye. *Proc. Geol. Assoc.*, vol. xlv, pt. 4, pp. 389–406.

1934a. J. Pringle and W. Manson. *In* Summary of Progress for 1933, Part I (*Mem. Geol. Surv.*), p. 83.

1942. R. M. MacLennan and A. E. Trueman. Variation in *Gryphaea incurva* (Sowerby) from the Lower Lias of Loch Aline, Morvern. *Proc. Roy. Soc. Edin.*, B, vol. lxi, pp. 211–232.

1942a. A. E. Trueman. A Note on the Base of the Lias near Broadford, Skye. *Trans. Geol. Soc. Glasgow*, vol. xx, pt. ii, pp. 205–207.

1945. E. B. Bailey. Tertiary Igneous Tectonics of Rhum (Inner Hebrides). *Quart. Journ. Geol. Soc.*, vol. c for 1944, pp. 165–188.

1948. F. W. Anderson. Isle of Skye. *Internat. Geol. Congress, 18th Session, Gt. Brit.* 1948. *Guide to Excursion A*13. (13 pp.).

1948a. F. W. ANDERSON. Algal Beds in the Great Estuarine Series of Skye. *Proc. Roy. Phys. Soc. Edin.*, vol. xiii, pp. 123–141.

1948b. F. W. ANDERSON and L. R. COX. The ' Loch Staffin Beds ' of Skye; with Notes on the Molluscan Fauna of the Great Estuarine Series. *Proc. Roy. Phys. Soc. Edin.*, vol. xiii, pp. 103–122.

1948c. TENG-CHIEN YEN. Some Bathonian Mollusca from Skye. *Geol. Mag.*, vol. lxxxv, pp. 167–171.

1949. R. M. MACLENNAN. A Starfish from the Glass Sand of Lochaline. *Geol. Mag.*, vol. lxxxvi, pp. 94–96.

1954. R. M. MACLENNAN. The Liassic Sequence in Morvern. *Trans. Geol. Soc. Glasgow*, vol. xxi, pt. iii, pp. 447–455.

1960. C. G. ADAMS. A Note on the Age of the Laig Gorge Beds, Eigg. *Geol. Mag.*, vol. xcvii, pp. 322–325 (Cretaceous).

1960a. J. D. HUDSON. The Laig Gorge Beds, Isle of Eigg. *Geol. Mag.*, vol. xcvii, pp. 313–322 (Cretaceous).

See also list of Geological Survey Memoirs on p. 120: West-Central Skye; Staffa, Iona and W. Mull; Pre-Tertiary Geology of Mull, Loch Aline and Oban; Arran; Ardnamurchan etc.

ADDITIONAL REFERENCES

1956. M. K. HOWARTH. The Scalpa Sandstone of the Isle of Raasay, Inner Hebrides. *Proc. Yorks. Geol. Soc.*, vol. 30, pp. 353–370.

1959. I. H. FORSYTH. A Marine Shell-Bed near the Base of the Estuarine Series in Raasay. *Trans. Edin. Geol. Soc.*, vol. 7, pt. 3, pp. 273–275.

1960. S. M. SMITH. Metamorphism of the Jurassic Rocks of Glas Bheinn Bheag, near Dunan, Isle of Skye. *Geol. Mag.*, vol. xcvii, pp. 466–479.

1961. A. HALLAM. Cyclothems, Transgressions and Formal change in the Lias of North-West Europe. *Trans. Edin. Geol. Soc.*, vol. 18, pt. 2, pp. 124–174.

1961a. D. W. HUMPHRIES. The Upper Cretaceous White Sandstone of Loch Aline, Argyll, Scotland. *Proc. Yorks. Geol. Soc.*, vol. 33, pp. 47–76.

1962. J. D. HUDSON. The Stratigraphy of the Great Estuarine Series (Middle Jurassic) of the Inner Hebrides. *Trans. Edin. Geol. Soc.*, vol. 19, pt. 2, pp. 139–165.

1963. P. McL. D. DUFF and C. M. BRUCK. A Jurassic Age for a Sedimentary Sequence on the Ben Hiant, Ardnamurchan, Argyll. *Trans. Edin. Geol. Soc.*, vol. 19, pt. 3, pp. 323–324.

IV. TERTIARY IGNEOUS ROCKS: INTRODUCTION AND PLATEAU LAVAS

1. INTRODUCTION

THERE IS NO greater contrast in the geography of Great Britain than that between its two main areas of Tertiary rocks. The comparatively low-lying and thickly populated country in the south-east of England, formed of Eocene and later deposits, is strikingly different from the jagged peaks and sparsely peopled Highland glens of the Tertiary igneous districts of Western Scotland. Yet these areas presented still more remarkable contrasts during the Tertiary period itself.

At the close of Cretaceous times the chalky oozes that covered much, if not all, of the British Isles were upheaved to form land, and were eroded in varying degrees. Soon, however, the sea again entered the region and extended over the south-eastern parts of England where inshore and estuarine deposits were laid down. In contrast, volcanic activity broke out to the north-west on a more extensive scale perhaps than any previously experienced in Britain.

The Tertiary igneous rocks are restricted mainly to the Inner Hebrides, Arran and North-east Ireland, though the products of the Tertiary volcanoes must have accumulated over a much wider area than that covered by the remnants now left. The earliest volcanic rocks, mainly basalt lavas, were poured out over a land-surface and were piled up, flow upon flow, to form mountains of great height. In the island of Mull there still remains a thickness of no less than 6,000 ft. of these rocks, in spite of prolonged denudation since the eruptions ceased. Yet the disconnected patches of lavas between Skye and Ireland indicate only a small part of the region affected. North-westwards, over the wide area now mainly occupied by the North Atlantic, the volcanic land no doubt continued, and embraced the Faeröes, Iceland, Greenland and the island of Jan Mayen (Fig. 17). The North Atlantic or Thulean igneous province also stretched westwards of Britain. Dredging has brought up from the Rockall Bank fragments of basalts like those of Scotland, and from the Porcupine Bank specimens of olivine-gabbro, while an intrusion forming the Rockall islet resembles in rock-type certain Tertiary masses in the west of Scotland (pp. 103, 106).

The eruption of the basalt lavas was followed by another kind of volcanic activity. Explosion-vents, mainly due to the uprise of an acid (rhyolitic) magma, are distributed at various places along the western seaboard of Scotland and are again encountered in North-east Ireland. The vents, which were of large size, were followed and in some cases preceded by the intrusion of plutonic masses. Within the limited areas thus marked out, the focus of activity shifted slightly from one point to another as time went on. Around each focus, or centre of intrusion, many assemblages of intrusive rocks were successively formed. During this long era intrusion was probably accompanied by extrusion, but of this there is little direct evidence. The intrusive complexes are situated in the high mountainous districts of the Inner Hebrides, Skye, Rum, Ardnamurchan and Mull, and also in Arran and North-east Ireland (Fig. 2). North-westerly extending fissures were formed from time to time, as is shown by the occurrence of a great series of basic dykes. The dykes traverse not only the basalt lavas and the Tertiary intrusive masses, but also the older rocks of Britain, over an area stretching from the Outer Hebrides and the western coast

41

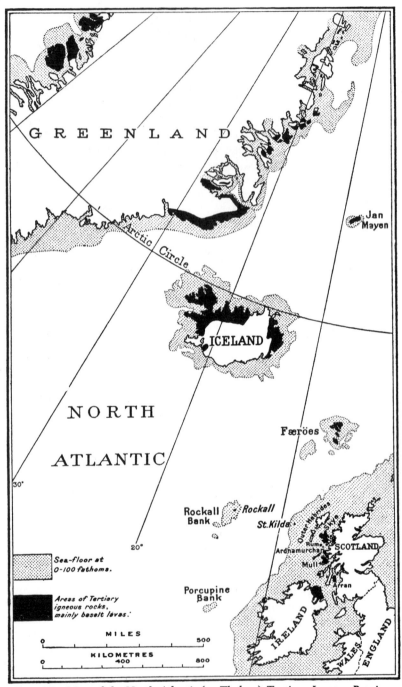

FIG. 17. *Map of the North Atlantic (or Thulean) Tertiary Igneous Province*

of Donegal south-eastwards to Yorkshire and the English Midlands. Widespread though they are, the dykes are found to be arranged in an orderly manner, being arranged in a number of linear swarms. Each swarm passes through one of the plutonic districts, north-westerly swarms being related to Skye, Mull and Arran in Scotland, and to the Carlingford–Slieve Gullion area and the Mourne Mountains in Ireland (Fig. 2). Other dykes, forming radial swarms, extend for short distances outwards from the centres of the plutonic complexes of Rum (Fig. 50) and of the Cuillin Hills in Skye.

Two contrasted explanations have been advanced to account for the distribution of the basalt lavas and the succeeding major intrusions. J. W. Judd, in 1874, suggested that the local intrusive complexes represent the ' basal wrecks ' of great volcanoes, from which the lavas had been erupted (1874)*. Sir Archibald Geikie, on the other hand, argued that the far-extending basaltic lava-plateau had been built up by eruptions from some of the widely distributed dyke-fissures (1897). He compared the British area to other extensive basaltic tracts, such as Iceland, where fissure-eruptions have actually occurred within historic times, and the plains of Idaho in the Western States of America. More recently however, evidence has been obtained, during the mapping of the island of Mull by the Geological Survey, of the existence of a great volcanic crater six miles in diameter in the centre of the island. The crater was in existence during the latter half of the basalt lava period, and so far Judd's great conception is justified. The north-west dyke-swarms are evidently causally related to the plutonic districts through which they pass, for the component dykes are particularly abundant in the immediate vicinity of these districts, to which indeed, acid dykes are practically confined. Not only Mull but also other plutonic districts were marked out as centres of igneous activity and as sites of magma-reservoirs *before* the intrusion of the dyke-swarms. Further, the majority of the north-westerly basic dykes come much too late in the time-scale to be considered as feeders for the lavas. It is, therefore, not improbable that the lavas were derived mainly from volcanic craters, almost all traces of which have been obliterated by the later-intruded plutonic masses. At any rate, it can be demonstrated that subsequently to the basaltic period great explosion vents were located in every plutonic district along the western coast of Scotland. Without doubt the line of plutonic complexes extending from Skye southwards to Slieve Gullion represents a chain of extinct volcanoes (*see also* 1937, 1937a).

Other centres of igneous activity were situated farther west. One of them is presumably represented in the St. Kilda group of islands that lies near the edge of the Continental submarine shelf west of the Outer Hebrides. Farther south, there are two marked concentrations of north-west dykes unrelated to any visible plutonic centre in their vicinity. One of these swarms crosses Islay, the other, of which less is known, traverses the western coast of Donegal. It is believed that they indicate the existence of two plutonic complexes, hidden beneath the waters of the Atlantic. Southwards, again, the olivine-gabbro dredged from the Porcupine Bank (Fig. 17) suggests that the bank marks the position of yet another plutonic complex.

A study has recently been made of the remanent magnetization of a large suite of specimens of Skye lavas and dykes and of some samples of gabbro from Skye, Rum and Ardnamurchan. Stably magnetized rocks show reverse magnetization. It is tentatively inferred that these Tertiary igneous rocks

---

* Dates within brackets refer to References on p. 53.

were formed during one general period (? Lower Miocene) when the Earth's magnetic field was reversed and the position of the North Pole was significantly different from its present location (1960).

2. PLATEAU LAVAS

(a) **General Description.** In the region of the Inner Hebrides the plateau lavas are now restricted to a few islands and promontories from Skye southwards to Mull. In Arran they occur only as small remnants within the Tertiary vent, in which down-slipped masses of Mesozoic strata are also found (p. 108). The extent of their outcrops is as follows:

	Sq. mls.
Island of Skye	425
Island of Raasay	1
The Small Isles (Rum, Eigg, Canna, Sanday, Muck)	18
Ardnamurchan	6
Island of Mull	280
Morvern	45
Island of Arran	—
TOTAL	775

In addition, there is a still wider tract (1,480 sq. miles) in North-east Ireland.

Each flow typically consists of a lower solid portion, often with a thin basal layer of slag, and an upper thick layer of slag. The solid basalt is crossed by vertical joints, caused by contraction during cooling, which in places divide the rock into six-sided columns (hexagonal, columnar or prismatic jointing). The columnar lavas may consist of three portions, or tiers. A lower tier of upright hexagonal columns is succeeded by a middle tier in which the columns are irregularly arranged and are much slighter than those below. The middle tier is surmounted by a layer of slag. The gas cavities (vesicles) of the slags are filled with minerals, forming amygdales. The minerals include various kinds of zeolites together with chlorite, chalcedony, quartz, calcite, etc. They are considered to have been deposited at a late stage in the consolidation of the lava from hot hydrous solutions (hydrothermal stage).

Around the coasts of the Inner Hebrides magnificent cliff-sections show the basalt lavas piled one upon another. The flows are often about 50 ft. in thickness, but many are thinner, while a few attain to 100 ft. or more. The individual flows can be followed by the eye along the cliffs, and are rarely seen to die out. No doubt each covered a large area. For example, a flow of basalt distinguished from adjoining flows by containing porphyritic feldspar has been traced throughout the plateau of Morvern over a distance of thirteen miles. For the most part the Hebridean plateau is built up of a monotonous series of olivine-basalts, and the extent of individual flows can rarely be ascertained.

The plateau country is typified by its scenery, consisting for the most part of low, broad hills, table-topped, with the hillsides terraced by step or trap features (Figs. 3, 22). Weathering has acted differentially upon the lava-pile, and the softer slag has been eroded more easily than the solid basalt, which forms rocky scarps along the edges of the flat-topped steps, or terraces.

The lavas were erupted quietly and intermittently. They are rarely inter-bedded with ash. Their upper parts are usually stained red by weathering and are frequently overlain by a layer or bed of red earth or bole, which also often occurs in cracks in the slaggy lava-tops. In the Inner Hebrides beds of bole up to a few feet in thickness have been recorded, but there are no deposits of iron-ore or of bauxitic clay like those which have been exploited commercially in the Tertiary plateau of Co. Antrim. Red clays analysed from Skye show a concentration of ferric iron of 13 to 38 per cent.

The red clays indicate that terrestrial conditions prevailed during the lava-period. Also, there is evidence of the occurrence of lakes and forests. In Ardnamurchan and Morvern sedimentary beds are occasionally seen below the basal lava; in Mull, Skye and elsewhere sediments are occasionally inter-stratified with the lavas. The sediments include seams of impure coal (lignite), leaf-beds, sandstones and conglomerates. The best known occurrence is at Ardtun in South-western Mull (Fig. 6). Fossil pollen grains of *Nelumbium* (lotus lily), *Magnolia* and species of Proteaceae are present in the pre-basaltic coal-seam and these would indicate at least a sub-tropical climate in the period preceding the volcanic onset. In the inter-basaltic beds of Ardtun and elsewhere leaves of *Ginkgo* (maiden-hair tree), *Platanus* (plane), *Corylites* (hazel), *Quercus* (oak) and

FIG. 18. *Fossil Tree, 40 ft. in height, submerged in Columnar Basalt Lava, South of Rudha na h-Uamha, Western Mull*

[Rep. from 'The Geology of Staffa, Iona and Western Mull' (*Mem. Geol. Surv.*), 1925 Fig. 8]

others, and pollen grains of numerous conifers and angiosperms suggest a climate perhaps slightly cooler than that of the pre-basaltic era, but still comparable with that of the northern Mediterranean coast to-day. The flora is comparable with Lower Tertiary floras of Greenland and other Arctic regions, and it was long thought that the beds are of Eocene date.

More recent evidence has been provided by fossil pollen from coal-bearing beds below and not far above the base of the lava sequence in Ardnamurchan and Mull; it suggests that the volcanic eruptions began not earlier than the Lower Oligocene and that most of the lavas are considerably younger—probably of late Miocene age (1951).

The Duke of Argyll, who first described the Ardtun deposits, drew attention to the absence of trunks or large branches, and concluded that the trees shed their leaves into the smooth still waters of some shallow lake (1851). An actual tree trunk was discovered by J. Maculloch embedded in lava along coastal cliffs south-west of The Wilderness in Western Mull (1819). The trunk is represented by a cast infilled with ' white trap ' (i.e. bleached basalt) and charred wood, 5 ft. across and 40 ft. in height, which is surrounded by remarkable columnar basalt (Fig. 18). The earliest record of volcanic activity in Skye is provided by a series of tuffs and sandy sediments, often with lignite, which underlie the first continuous lava flows. They are primarily palagonite tuffs laid down in shallow lakes on the old Tertiary land surface. North of Portree they attain a thickness of 120 ft. and include large lava ' bombs ', impersistent lava flows, fragments of wood and planty sediments. *Gingko* was one of the plants identified from these beds. Similar, but much thinner, intercalations occur at higher levels in the lava series, one of which in Glen Osdale has yielded a flora similar to that of Ardtun and which includes *Quercus*, *Corylus* and *Platanus* (1935–40).

(b) **Mull, Morvern and Ardnamurchan.** The sequence of the plateau lavas in Mull (1924), including lavas and sediments, is as follows (*see* Plate III):

TERTIARY PLATEAU LAVAS:

2. Central Group:
olivine-poor basalts, upwards of 3,000 ft. thick, within and around a lava-caldera. Pillow-lavas frequent within caldera.

> Porphyritic feldspathic, and non-porphyritic, with variolitic types forming pillow-lavas.

1. Plateau Group:
mainly olivine-rich basalts, 3,000 ft. thick.

> c. ' Pale ' suite of Ben More: olivine-basalts, with a horizon of mugearite and big-feldspar basalt near base.
> b. Main suite: olivine-basalts.
> a. Staffa suite: columnar olivine-poor tholeiitic basalts.

TERTIARY SEDIMENTS:

2. Intercalations between lava-flows.

> Red boles, due to sub-aerial decay of lava-tops. Plant-beds, lignites, and conglomerates of South-west Mull.

1. Basal Deposits.

> b. Basal Mudstone, probably decomposed ash, underlain (in South-east Mull) by Flint Conglomerate.
> a. Desert Sand, penetrating fissures in the Chalk in West Mull (Gribun).

The basal mudstone is found throughout Mull, Morvern and Ardnamurchan, and is remarkably continuous for so thin a deposit. In Ardnamurchan, near Ardslignish, it is underlain by a coal-seam.

The Plateau Group is present in its full development only in Western Mull. Elsewhere, wherever the base of the group is exposed, the tholeiitic lavas characteristic of the Staffa suite are absent. The Pale suite of Ben More is almost wholly unrepresented in the eastern parts of the island, where the horizon of the mugearite and big-feldspar basalt is almost directly succeeded by lavas of the Central Group. It is noteworthy that the columnar lavas of Staffa and the west of Mull are identical in structure and composition with the upper group of the basalt lavas in Antrim, as developed at the Giant's Causeway.

In Morvern the Plateau Group consists of some 1,500 ft. of olivine-basalt lavas, with an extensive and massive flow of basalt with porphyritic feldspars near or at the base (p. 44), and with composite flows of mugearite and big-feldspar basalt towards the top. In Ardnamurchan the lavas have been largely denuded away, their maximum thickness, near Ardslignish, being 300 ft. Large masses, however, occur down-faulted within volcanic vents of later date.

The Central Group is found only in Central and South-eastern Mull, where it persists owing to subsidences that took place during the basaltic period and after its close. In Central Mull, within a subsidence-caldera, six miles in diameter, a thick series of these lavas include many examples of pillow-lava. They occur in patches isolated from one another by the later intrusive masses. From the observed dips of these lava-remnants it is concluded that stratigraphically higher flows are situated towards the centre of the area. A succession consisting of three zones has been made out, as follows:

3. Central Zone: very compact non-porphyritic basalts of Central type (olivine-poor or olivine-free).

2. Middle Zone: highly porphyritic basalts of Central type, crowded with feldspar phenocrysts.

1. Outer Zone: Central types of basalt often ill-developed; an approach to the olivine-rich Plateau type frequent.

Pillow-lavas of variolitic basalt occur in the outer and middle zones (1 and 2), but are absent from the central zone (3). Pillow-structure is a feature of lavas that have flowed into standing water, and the examples from the interior of Mull indicate the repeated occurrence of lakes formed during the periods of quiescence within a vast crater (Fig. 19). The floor of this wide crater, or caldera, sank repeatedly. This is indicated by the great thickness of the pillow-lava assemblage. Also, it is noteworthy that explosion-vents of later date, which pierce the caldera, are filled with Tertiary igneous rocks and contain practically no fragments of Mesozoic sediments or of Moine Gneiss; whereas, outside the caldera, vents contain these pre-Tertiary rocks in abundance. It would appear that the pre-Tertiary ' floor ' within the limits of the caldera and also within a much later caldera to the north-west had sunk, and so far down its materials were not carried up to the present level by the vent-explosions.

Lavas of the Central Group still persist outside the limits of the lava-caldera in the cores of concentric folds that surround Central Mull (p. 63). They consist of basalts of Central types like those found within the caldera (except that variolites are absent), and no doubt they are all of the same general age. No upper limit to the Central Group is seen, and the group is not exposed elsewhere in the Hebrides.

In addition to the great central basaltic crater of Mull, smaller vents occur

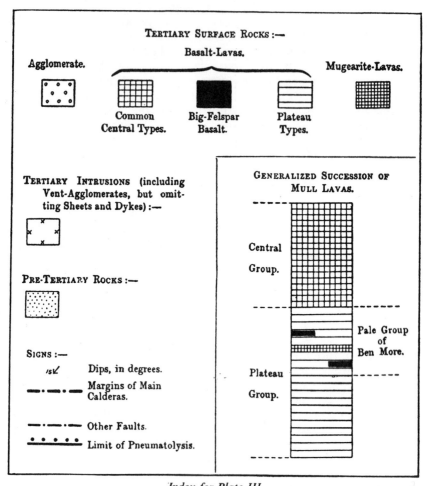

Index for Plate III

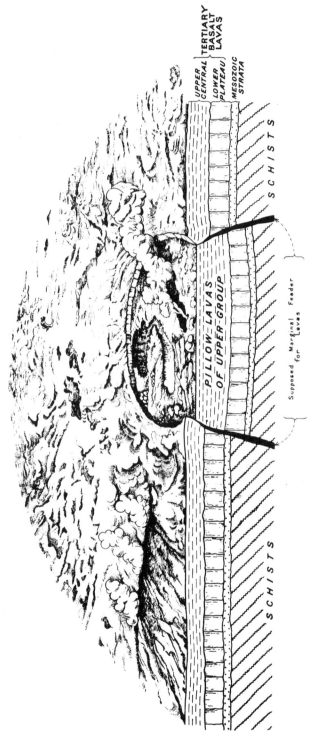

FIG. 19. *Reconstruction of the Basaltic Volcano of Central Mull, in Bird's-eye View and Section*

which may have been active during the basalt lava period. A few examples may be given. In Central Mull a line of plugs of dolerite with feldspar phenocrysts extends from the northern end of Loch Spelve north-westwards for over six miles. In Northern Mull, at 'S Airdhe Bheinn and Loch Frisa, there are plugs of olivine-dolerite. Trachyte plugs piercing basaltic agglomerate are also found in Northern Mull (Salen, Ardnacross).

(c) **Skye and the Small Isles of Inverness-shire.** In Skye, in Raasay, and in Rum, Eigg, Canna, Sanday and Muck, to the south, olivine-basalt lavas identical

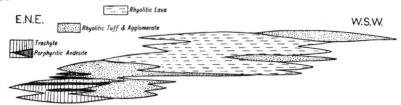

FIG. 20. *Diagrammatic Representation of the Relations of the Trachytic and Rhyolitic Lavas and Tuffs of Fionn Choire, Cuillin Hills, Skye*
[Rep. from *Tertiary Skye Memoir*, 1904, Fig. 9]

with the Plateau type of Mull are parts of an extensive if deeply eroded plateau. In Skye 2,000 ft. of these lavas are exposed (1904). In the area around the Cuillin Hills, other lava-types have been recognized. A few olivine-free flows have been described as andesitic (1904). Porphyritic basalts with abundant phenocrysts of labradorite feldspar occur on the Talisker cliffs on the western coast, and resemble basalts of the Central Group of Mull, though they are clearly associated with the Plateau Group. A thick series of intermediate and acid lavas occurs on the northern side of the Cuillins. The series is exposed for a vertical distance of 2,000 ft., and consists of the following groups (Fig. 20):

3. Rhyolite lavas.
2. Rhyolitic tuff and agglomerates.
1. Trachyte lavas, with interbedded flows of porphyritic andesite.

The above groups interdigitate with one another and with the basalt lavas on their flanks. The series is intercalated in the Plateau Group, for the rhyolites (3) are overlain by basalts. The vent or vents from which this locally developed suite of lavas and agglomerates were erupted are believed to have lain within the Cuillin Hills.

Mugearite, and mugearitic basalt with large feldspar phenocrysts, have long been known to form a number of composite sheets near Mugeary, Druim na Criche and Roineval, some six miles N.N.W. of the Cuillin Hills. These sheets were originally regarded as sills (1904) but more recently have been shown to be composite lava-flows (1931). During the subsequent survey of Northern Skye (*see* 1935–40), mugearite and mugearitic basalt lavas, some with large porphyritic feldspars (' big-feldspar-basalts '), along with subordinate trachytes, were found to accompany olivine-basalts in a belt, from five to three miles wide, extending from the Loch Harport–Roineval–Druim na Criche area for twelve miles north-westwards to the vicinity of Loch Greshornish. A few porphyritic and non-porphyritic mugearite lavas also occur locally in the vicinity of Portree, in Duirinish and in Vaternish, and non-porphyritic mugearite lava forms cappings on the great lava escarpment, between Hartaval and Beinn Edra in Trotternish. Feldspar-phyric basalt lavas are interbedded with non-porphyritic basalt flows in Duirinish and north of Dunvegan.

The survey of Northern Skye has shown that a ' Great Group of Basic Sills ' intruded in the lavas (1904) does not, in fact, exist. These alleged sills in Skye, as in Mull (1924) and elsewhere·in the Hebridean region, are the hard, columnar centres of lava-flows. Oligoclase-basalt lavas similar to Skye mugarites are known in many parts of the world and their nomenclature has been the subject of comment (1952a, 1954).

Early eruptions in Skye were responsible for the formation of basaltic tuffs (including palagonite tuffs which locally contain fragments of fossil wood) and agglomerates. At the base of the plateau-lavas such materials occur near Portree and in Vaternish (palagonite tuffs) and on the north side of the Sound of Soay (bedded agglomerate). Isolated masses of agglomerate, with fragments of gabbro, granite, etc., are found within the plutonic area. South-east of the granite and granophyre masses of the Red Hills, at Kilchrist, a large vent contains fragments of felsite, granophyre, gabbro, basalt and pre-Tertiary sediments, and has been referred to the earlier part of the basaltic period (1904). The local presence of ignimbrite has recently been inferred (1960a).

In Raasay, the lavas occupy much of the area north of Dun Caan that is shown on Fig. 13 as ' dolerite and basalt ' (1935).

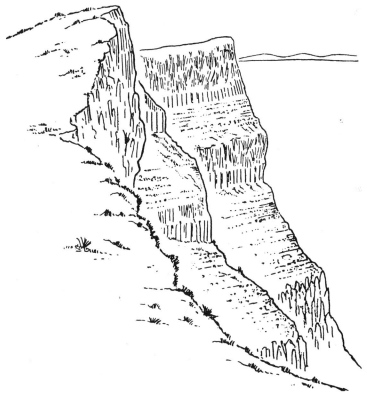

FIG. 21. *View of Cliff at Compass Hill, Canna, showing Bedded Conglomerates and Tuffs with Sheets of Columnar ' Dolerite '*
[Rep. from ' The Geology of the Small Isles of Inverness-shire ' (*Mem. Geol. Surv.*), 1908, Fig. 10]

In the Small Isles of Inverness-shire agglomerates and conglomerates are interstratified with one another near the base of the basaltic plateau (1908). The

FIG. 22. *View of Lava-plateau of Eigg, with the Sgùrr (formed of Pitchstone)*
[Rep. from 'The Geology of the Small Isles of Inverness-shire' (*Mem. Geol. Surv.*), 1908, Fig. 16]

occurrence of the conglomerates suggests that a great river traversed the basaltic plateau. At Compass Hill, on the east coast of the Isle of Canna, a cliff, 450 ft. in height, affords a magnificent section of these beds (Fig. 21). Sheets of columnar ' dolerite ' traversing the cliff are now regarded as lava-flows. The fragmental deposits thin out to a few feet on the northern and western coasts of Canna, and to the south, on the adjacent island of Sanday. In addition to basalt, the deposits contain pebbles of gneiss, schist, Torridonian grit, etc., and plants and pieces of charred wood are also found. On the island of Rum lava forms four small outliers. Tuff or volcanic conglomerate with pebbles of basalt, gneiss, granophyre, Torridonian grit, etc. occurs locally at the base of the succession and in one outlier volcanic conglomerate also occupies a higher horizon (1952). Again, on the island of Eigg, not very far above the base of the volcanic succession, fragmental deposits with pieces of basalt, Jurassic sandstone, wood, etc., occur between basaltic lavas and a great sheet of pitch-stone that forms the well-known Sgùrr. These fragmental materials in Eigg have been interpreted as river-deposits and as vent-agglomerates by different observers (*see* below).

In the basaltic plateau of the Small Isles the lavas remaining are probably between 1,000 and 2,000 ft. in thickness. Olivine-basalts are prevalent, as in other parts of the Inner Hebrides. In addition, mugearite lavas occur in Rum, where they comprise about 40 per cent of the thickness of a basalt/mugearite succession (1942, 1942a, 1952), and in Eigg, Muck and Canna.

The great columnar sheet of pitchstone that forms the Sgùrr of Eigg has been the subject of some controversy (Fig. 22). Sir Archibald Geikie in the first instance supposed that the pitchstone represented a series of subaerial lava-flows, occupying a system of valleys eroded in the basaltic plateau (1897). Later, A. Harker came to the conclusion that the whole mass was an intrusive sheet, and showed that it was itself intruded by numerous thin sheets of felsite, which represented intrusions of the pitchstone magma into the earlier-consolidated pitchstone (1908). More recently E. B. Bailey, while agreeing that the bedded aspect of the pitchstone was due to auto-intrusion, supported Geikie's main conception, that the pitchstone flowed down a river-valley (1914). Harker, in replying, directed attention to the smooth nature of the contact between the base of the pitchstone and the supposed eroded side of the valley as being unlike the terraced hill-slopes of the plateau country of the present day (1914a; *see also* 1929).

REFERENCES

1819. J. MacCulloch. *A Description of the Western Islands of Scotland.* London. (Vol. i, p. 568).
1851. Duke of Argyll. On Tertiary Leaf-Beds in the Isle of Mull. *Quart. Journ. Geol. Soc.*, vol. vii, pp. 89–103.
1874. J. W. Judd. The Secondary Rocks of Scotland. Second Paper. On the Ancient Volcanoes of the Highlands and the Relations of their Products to the Mesozoic Strata. *Quart. Journ. Geol. Soc.*, vol. xxx, pp. 220–301.
1887. J. Starkie Gardner. On the Leaf-Beds and Gravels of Ardtun, Carsaig, etc. in Mull. *Quart. Journ. Geol. Soc.*, vol. xliii, pp. 270–300.
1897. Sir Archibald Geikie. *The Ancient Volcanoes of Great Britain.* Vol. ii. London.
1899. M. F. Heddle. The Minerals of the Storr. *Trans. Edin. Geol. Soc.*, vol. vii, pt. iv, pp. 328–331.

1904. A. HARKER. The Tertiary Igneous Rocks of Skye. *Mem. Geol. Surv.*

1908. A. HARKER. The Geology of the Small Isles of Inverness-shire. *Mem. Geol. Surv.*

1914. E. B. BAILEY. The Sgùrr of Eigg. *Geol. Mag.*, dec. vi, vol. i, pp. 296–305.

1914a. A. HARKER. The Sgùrr of Eigg: some Comments on Mr. Bailey's Paper. *Geol. Mag.*, dec. vi, vol. i, pp. 306–308.

1915. W. F. P. McLINTOCK. On the Zeolites and Associated Minerals of the Tertiary Lavas around Ben More, Mull. *Trans. Roy. Soc. Edin.*, vol. li, pt. i, pp. 1–33.

1924. E. B. BAILEY and others. The Tertiary and Post-Tertiary Geology of Mull, Loch Aline and Oban. *Mem. Geol. Surv.*

1929. S. H. REYNOLDS. The Isle of Eigg. *Geography*, June No. (8 pp.).

1931. W. Q. KENNEDY. On Composite Lava Flows. *Geol. Mag.*, vol. lxviii, pp. 166–181.

1935. C. F. DAVIDSON. The Tertiary Geology of Raasay, Inner Hebrides. *Trans. Roy. Soc. Edin.*, vol. lviii, pt. ii, pp. 375–407.

1935–40. G. V. WILSON and others. *In* Summaries of Progress of the Geological Survey (*Mems. Geol. Surv.*): for 1934, Pt. I, pp. 70–71; for 1935, Pt. I,. pp. 81–84; for 1936, Pt. I, pp. 77–79; for 1937, pp. 73–74; for 1938, pp. 74–76.

1937. J. E. RICHEY. Some Features of Tertiary Volcanicity in Scotland and Ireland. *Bull. Volcanol.*, sér. ii, tome i, pp. 13–34.

1937a. G. W. TYRRELL. Flood Basalts and Fissure Eruption. *Bull. Volcanol.*, sér. ii, tome i, pp. 89–111.

1940. J. E. RICHEY. Association of Explosive Brecciation and Plutonic Intrusion in the British Tertiary Igneous Province. *Bull. Volcanol.*, ser. ii, tome vi, pp. 157–175.

1942. S. I. TOMKEIEFF. The Tertiary Lavas of Rum. *Geol. Mag.*, vol. lxxix, pp. 1–13.

1942a. S. I. TOMKEIEFF and K. B. BLACKBURN. On the Remains of Fossil Wood enclosed in a Tertiary Lava on the Isle of Rum, Inner Hebrides. *Geol. Mag.*, vol. lxxix, pp. 14–17.

1948. F. W. ANDERSON. *In* Skye and Morar. *Internat. Geol. Congress, 18th Session, Gt. Brit. 1948. Guide to Excursion* C14, pp. 6–8.

1951. J. B. SIMPSON. The Age of Tertiary Vulcanicity in Scotland. *British. Assoc. for Adv. Sci., Edinburgh Meeting Programme*, p. 63.

1952. G. P. BLACK. The Tertiary Volcanic Succession of the Isle of Rhum, Inverness-shire. *Trans. Edin. Geol. Soc.*, vol. xv, pp. 39–51.

1952a. F. WALKER. Mugearites and Oligoclase-Basalts. *Geol. Mag.*, vol. lxxxix, pp. 337–345.

1954. A. K. WELLS. Mugearites and Oligoclase-Basalts. *Geol. Mag.*, vol. xci, pp. 14–16.

1957. R. C. MACKENZIE. Saponite from Allt Ribhein, Fiskavaig Bay, Skye. *Mineralogical Mag.*, vol. xxxi, pp. 672–680.

1959. J. M. SWEET. A Re-examination of Uigite. *Mineralogical Mag.*, vol. xxxii, pp. 340–342.

1960. M. AFTAB KHAN. The Remanent Magnetization of the Basic Tertiary Igneous Rocks of Skye, Inverness-shire. *Geophys. Journ. Roy. Astronom. Soc.*, vol. 3, no. 1, pp. 45–62.

1960a. P. S. RAY. Ignimbrite in the Kilchrist Vent, Skye. *Geol. Mag.*, vol. xcvii, pp. 229–238.

See also list of Geological Survey Memoirs on p. 120: West-Central Skye; Glenelg, Lochalsh and S.E. Skye; Staffa, Iona and W. Mull; Ardnamurchan etc.

1961. I. D. MUIR and C. E. Tilley. Mugearites and their place in Alkali Igneous Rock Series. *Journ. Geol.*, vol. 69, pp. 186–203.

1962. C. E. TILLEY and I. D. MUIR. The Hebridean Plateau Magma Type. *Trans. Edin. Geol. Soc.*, vol. 19, pt. 2, pp. 208–215.

See also list of Geological Survey Memoirs on p. 120: West-Central Skye; Glenelg, Lochalsh and S. E. Skye; Staffa, Iona and W. Mull; Ardnamurchan, etc.

V. TERTIARY IGNEOUS ROCKS: CENTRAL INTRUSION COMPLEXES

1. INTRODUCTION

(*a*) **General Sequence.** The mapping of the plutonic centres of the Inner Hebrides and Arran by the Geological Survey has disclosed in each district a complexity of volcanic vents and intrusions which mark an igneous cycle of unsurpassed magnitude and variety. Also, the intrusions display an orderliness in their structure and arrangement which permits of conclusions of great importance as to their ultimate shapes and the methods of emplacement of the magmas concerned.

Our knowledge of the igneous cycle has made striking progress since the mapping of the region was commenced. In Ireland the Tertiary plutonic districts of Carlingford, Slieve Gullion and the Mourne Mountains, together with the basaltic plateau of Antrim, were investigated by the Geological Survey at an early date, mainly between the years 1870 and 1880. Since the plutonic complexes lay to the south of the basaltic plateau, their time relations could not be directly determined, but a simple magmatic sequence, from basic to acid magma, with a final recurrence of basic magma, was suggested to explain the succession throughout the region (1895)*. In Scotland this view was modified during the survey of Skye and the Small Isles by A. Harker between the years 1893 and 1903. In these districts the conclusion was reached that, in general, different modes of occurrence of the igneous masses marked their order in time. Fragmental volcanic rocks were succeeded by the plateau basalts, and these by the plutonic rocks and finally by the minor intrusions. In the volcanic and plutonic phases the sequence was from basic to acid magmas, while in the phase of minor intrusions basic and acid magmas were first intruded at or about the same time, and were superseded finally by basic magma.

The investigation of the more central parts of the island of Mull during the six years prior to the outbreak of war in 1914, brought a new point of view, and modifications of the ideas based upon the rocks of Skye and Rum. Volcanic vents, minor intrusions and plutonic masses were found to alternate repeatedly with one another in no definite order, and only in a general way could it be said that there were magmatic cycles beginning with basic and ending with acid magmas. On the contrary, it was clear that both basic and acid magmas had often been available for intrusion at approximately the same time, a fact already recognized in Skye. Further, the igneous masses were found to be arranged in concentric series around certain points, called intrusion-centres. The existence of at least two centres of different ages was demonstrated, an earlier centre situated within the great lava-caldera from which the upper lavas of Mull had been erupted, and a later centre located a few miles farther to the north-west. In Ardnamurchan, which was surveyed in 1921–23, an even clearer demonstration of this principle was obtained. Altogether, three centres of intrusion were indicated by the mapping and were shown to have functioned successively. Again, in the island of Arran, mapped by W. Gunn between the years 1893 and 1900 and re-investigated more recently by G. W. Tyrrell and others, it has been

* Dates within brackets refer to References on p. 62.

found that there also the centre of igneous activity migrated from one point to another.

(*b*) **Types of Intrusion.** The intrusions related to the centres are of several distinct types. The position of the centre itself is indicated by rock-masses of annular or arcuate form, which are arranged in concentric series around the centre. Two types of concentric intrusions have been recognized, namely, *ring-dykes*, of plutonic dimensions and, in general, with coarse crystallization, and *cone-sheets*, which are minor intrusions usually of fine or medium grain. Volcanic *vents* of the explosive type are also distributed around many of the intrusion-centres. Linear dykes occur either in north-westerly directed *dyke-swarms* crossing the centrally related complexes or in groups aligned radially or tangentially to the centres (*radial* and *tangential swarms*). In addition, within the areas occupied by the other intrusions or distributed over the surrounding region, there are horizontal *sills*, inclined *sheets* and small *bosses* and *plugs*, which are not arranged as a rule in any orderly manner.

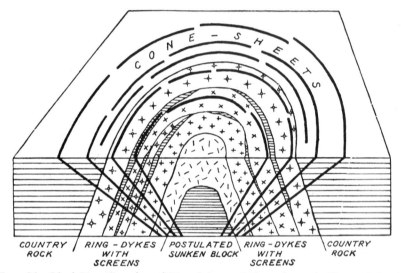

COUNTRY   RING - DYKES   POSTULATED   RING - DYKES   COUNTRY
ROCK   WITH   SUNKEN BLOCK   WITH   ROCK
            SCREENS   SCREENS

FIG. 23. *Ideal Ring Complex of Ring-dykes and Cone-sheets, in Plan and Section*
[Rep. with permission from ' Tertiary Ring Structures in Britain ', *Trans. Geol. Soc. Glasgow* vol. xix, pt. 1, 1932, Fig. 2]

Different conclusions have been reached in different areas in regard to the external form of the plutonic complexes, taken as a whole. Certain plutonic rock-assemblages in Skye and Rum have been considered to be *complex laccoliths*. In other districts the margins of individual masses of arcuate or annular shape are steeply transgressive to the older rocks in contact, and the masses are termed *ring-dykes*. A multiple mass built up of such intrusions resembles a *stock*. In gabbroic rocks, *banding* is notable in Rum (1960) and Skye.

A complex composed of ring-dykes and cone-sheets is typified in plan and section in Fig. 23, and this illustration may serve to show the essential features of these types of intrusion (1932, 1937, 1937*a*). The *ring-dykes* vary in width in different cases from about a hundred yards to a mile or more. The inclination of those of Tertiary age is, often at least, steeply outwards from the centre, as shown in Fig. 23. On the other hand, ring-dykes of cylindrical form are found in certain complexes, such as those of Glen Coe and Ben Nevis, which are of Lower Old Red Sandstone age.

It was from these complexes that evidence was first obtained concerning the mode of intrusion of ring-dykes. At Glen Coe a cylinder composed of Lower Old Red Sandstone lavas resting upon Highland Schists, bounded by a ring fault, has subsided for thousands of feet between walls composed of the schists. Simultaneously with the subsidence, it is concluded, magma rose up the circular fissure around the cylinder on, at any rate, two occasions, forming two ring-dykes of granite. It is considered probable that these or earlier rings of magma reached the surface and that a superficial caldera was formed, around and within which lava accumulated. The basaltic caldera of Mull, marked by a central area of subsidence, is another instance of this phenomenon (p. 47). A diagrammatic representation of these structures is given in Fig. 24. In some

SECTIONS SHOWING
CAULDRON SUBSIDENCES

SURFACE CALDERA AND RING-DYKES
(SHOWING SUPPOSED CONNECTION)

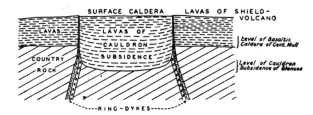

UNDERGROUND CAULDRON SUBSIDENCE

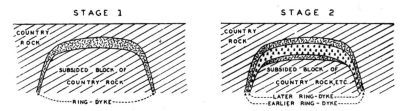

FIG. 24. *Diagrammatic Cross-sections of Cauldron Subsidences*

cases, however, a ring fault was connected by a cross-fracture before reaching the surface; an underground cauldron of subsidence was formed, magma rising and filling the cavity left between the subsiding block of country rock and its roof. Repeated subsidences of the first-formed block, together with portions of the earlier intrusions, are believed to constitute the mechanism for the formation of a complete ring-dyke complex. Examples are seen in Mull, Ardnamurchan and elsewhere, in which practically the entire area enclosed by the outermost ring-dyke is composed of plutonic rocks. In ring-dyke complexes it is often observed that successively younger intrusions are encountered as we proceed inwards towards the centre, and the theory of central subsidence supplies a reason for this arrangement. Often, however, ring-dykes in Mull and other

E

districts are separated by narrow wall-like strips of older rocks, which have been termed *screens*. In such cases the age relations of the ring-dykes concerned cannot be ascertained, unless the screen is discontinuous so that the two plutonic rocks come into direct contact with one another. It seems likely that a later ring-dyke fracture would tend to avoid the hard contact-altered wall of older rock bordering an earlier ring-dyke. To this the formation of the screens is perhaps mainly due.

Two more features are noteworthy. As a rule, ring-dyke complexes are not circular but are roughly oval in shape. A good example is provided by Centre 3, Ardnamurchan (Fig. 34). Further, the ring-dykes are often arranged somewhat eccentrically, and in such cases a complex is not symmetrical relatively to a single point, but possesses a plane of bilateral symmetry. An instance is the complex of ring-dykes around Beinn Chaisgidle in Mull (Fig. 29) with an axis of symmetry extending north-west to south-east.

Cone-sheets are inclined inwards and downwards towards a common focus, usually at angles of about 45 degrees. They form annular belts around centres that are also marked out by ring-dykes, and these belts enclose a central area free from sheet-intrusion. Only a few cone-sheets are drawn on Fig. 23, but usually they occur in great numbers (Figs. 31, 37). Though individual sheets are only a few feet or yards in width, cone-sheets collectively occupy large parts of the complexes of Mull and Ardnamurchan. The sheets were intruded successively, for each has well-chilled edges irrespective of whether they are in contact with country-rock or with earlier cone-sheets (*see also* 1937, 1937c).

The underground focus towards which cone-sheets are inclined is supposed to coincide with the top of a magma-reservoir from which the cone-sheet fissures were filled. In the case of the Cuillin Hills in Skye, the sheets near the interior of the cone-sheet belt are more steeply inclined than those near the periphery, and this rule also applies to two sets of sheets arranged around Centre 2 in Ardnamurchan. By projecting the latter cone-sheets downwards with their observed angles of inclination an approximate depth for the focus of about three miles is arrived at (Fig. 25); and the same depth is indicated by other Hebridean suites of cone-sheets. Not improbably, however, the cone-sheets do not continue with the inclinations observed at the surface, but curve downwards towards the reservoir, the top of which may therefore be situated at a somewhat greater depth than that inferred (1924, 1936a).

The volcanic *vents* due to explosion are naturally irregular in outline. They are in some cases elongate in shape and roughly disposed tangentially about the centre to which they are related. Vents around Slieve Gullion in Ireland, situated along a ring fissure later intruded by ring-dykes, are a case in point. The vents are in most cases due to the explosive energy of acid (rhyolite) or intermediate (trachyte) magma (1940). Their agglomerates and breccias are made up in part of such materials, and in part of pre-existing rocks traversed by the vents. Lavas of rhyolite and of andesitic pitchstone (inninmorite) are interbedded with the vent-agglomerates in certain areas. It has been suggested that the linear vent of Glas Eilean, near Kilchoan, Ardnamurchan (1940) provides evidence of ' fluidization ' (gas-transport of solid particles) having been involved in its emplacement, and that its tuff matrix is an ignimbrite (1954).

The *north-west swarms of linear dykes* have been already referred to, and will be dealt with in more detail in a later section (p. 111). *Radial dykes* diverging from intrusion-centres are developed in the Cuillin Hills in Skye and in Rum (Fig. 50); and *tangential dykes* are arranged around the Cuillin centre.

Sills are best seen traversing the Mesozoic strata underlying the plateau basalt lavas, and are a special feature of Skye and Arran. They are often massive intrusions, and when composed of acid materials they sometimes tend to be laccolithic in form.

Sills, dykes and cone-sheets frequently consist of two contrasted injections. In such *composite intrusions* the first injection consists of basic magma, which is chilled externally against the older rocks in contact, the second of a more acid magma, which intruded itself along the centre of the basic injection before the latter had completely consolidated, or at any rate before it had become cold. The internal contacts between basic and acid portions are therefore unchilled, and often one rock merges into the other or else the acid rock is flanked on either side by a hybrid zone formed by its admixture with basic materials. Since the two contrasted magmas were intruded at approximately the same time, it

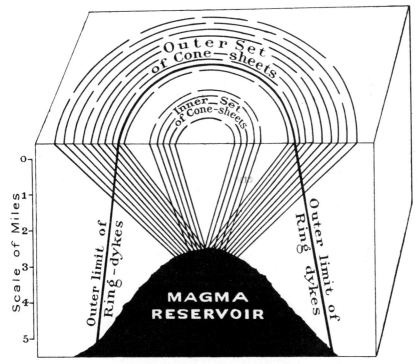

FIG. 25. *Diagram showing Cone-sheets of Centre 2, Ardnamurchan, in relation to inferred Magma-reservoir*
[Rep. from ' The Geology of Ardnamurchan ', etc. (*Mem. Geol. Surv.*), 1930, Fig. 5]

appears to follow, as A. Harker first pointed out (1904), that basic and acid magmas must have co-existed in the magma-reservoir from which they were both derived. To account for the basic magma being invariably intruded before the acid magma, it has been suggested by E. B. Bailey (1924) that the intrusion of the acid magma becomes possible only when the fissure has been warmed up by the injection of the more mobile and hotter basic magma.

(*c*) **Composition of Rocks.** The intrusive rocks may be referred mainly to a few rock-types. Among the plutonic masses, gabbro and granophyre or granite are prevalent. Gabbroic rocks with basic plagioclase feldspar (bytownite or anorthite), termed eucrite, are also frequent. Ultrabasic rocks, such as peridotite, picrite and allivalite (composed of olivine and anorthite) are found in plutonic masses, and also in minor intrusions. In the cone-sheets quartz-dolerite is most common, but there are also suites composed of dolerite with feldspar pheno-crysts, of olivine–dolerite and of more acid rocks, such as craignurite (an intermediate rock with acicular augite), granophyre and felsite. Among the dykes quartz-dolerite and tholeiite, olivine-dolerite and crinanite, are widespread, whereas acid types are almost entirely confined to the immediate vicinity of a plutonic district.

A consideration of the chemical compositions of the more important Tertiary igneous rocks has brought into prominence relationships existing between them. With reference to the rocks of Mull, E. B. Bailey and H. H. Thomas formulated a scheme for the classification of magmas based upon the chemical rock-analyses. In order to fix attention solely upon chemical composition, the term *magma-type* was employed to designate a chemical analysis, or set of closely similar analyses, although the equivalent rocks may possess distinct textural characters. Thus, analyses of volcanic, plutonic and hypabyssal rocks may fall within the same magma-type. The qualifying name given to a magma-type may have reference either to composition as regards silica-content or to a rock-type whose analysis typifies the magma-type. For example, there is the Acid Magma-Type, the Plateau Basalt (or Plateau) Magma-Type, etc.

A magma-type may be concluded to bear a lineal relationship to other magma-types, and such types are collectively regarded as constituting a *magma-series*. The most important magma-series recognized in the British Tertiary province are named the Normal Magma-Series, the Eucrite–Allivalite Magma-Series, and the Alkaline Magma-Series. An important magma-type not included in a magma-series is the Porphyritic Central Magma-Type.

Separation of early-formed crystals by gravity in a slowly cooled magma-reservoir was invoked as the main mechanism whereby various magma-types had been derived from parent stocks.

The Normal Magma-Series, as established in Mull, is a typical linear series, and includes in order of increasing acidity the Plateau Magma-Type, the Non-Porphyritic Central Magma-Type and various intermediate (andesitic) and sub-acid stages ending with the Acid Magma-Type. The Plateau and Non-Porphyritic Central Magma-Types are named respectively after the olivine-basalt lavas of the Plateau Group and the olivine-poor or olivine-free basalts of the Central Group of Mull.

The Porphyritic Central Magma-Type is exemplified by the basalt lavas with porphyritic feldspar belonging to the Central Group of Mull, and also by many intrusions of gabbro and quartz-gabbro of other districts. It is regarded as a derivative of the Non-Porphyritic Central Magma-Type by the enrichment of the magma in early-formed plagioclase feldspar with or without olivine. The Eucrite–Allivalite Magma-Series is supposed to have come from the Porphyritic Central Magma-Type by the accumulation of early-formed olivine and basic plagioclase feldspar.

The Alkaline Magma-Series is, for various reasons, considered to be descended from the Plateau Magma-Type. It includes, in order of increasing acidity, the Mugearite, Trachyte and Alkali-syenite Magma-Types.

A tree of descent can therefore be constructed to indicate the relationships between the various magma-types and magma-series.

Plateau Magma-Type   Non-Porphyritic Central Magma-Type

                Acid Magma-Type Porphyritic Central Magma-Type

Alkaline Magma-Series   Eucrite-Allivalite Magma-Series

The Plateau and Non-Porphyritic Central Magma-Types, renamed Olivine-basalt and Tholeiitic Magma-Types (respectively alkaline and calc-alkaline), are regarded by W. Q. Kennedy as parent magmas from which others have been derived (1933, 1938), whereas Bailey, Thomas (1924) and N. L. Bowen (1928) had supposed that the Non-Porphyritic Central Magma-Type is a derivative of the Plateau Magma-Type. More recently C. E. Tilley has suggested that in basaltic provinces a member of the Tholeiitic Magma-Series (tholeiitic picrite-basalt—tholeiitic olivine-basalt—hypersthene-basalt) may well be the parent magma from which the Alkali Magma-Series (olivine-basalt—mugearite —trachyte) is derived (1950). There has been much discussion of the meaning and correct use of the terms ' Magma-Type ' and ' Magma-Series ', ' alkaline ' and ' calc-alkaline ', ' tholeiite ' and ' tholeiitic ' (1948, 1949, 1949a, 1956).

A fundamentally different point of view in regard to the relationships of magmas has been advocated by A. Holmes (1931, 1936). In reviving Bunsen's conception of basic and acid ' earth-magmas ', Holmes supposes that the basaltic and granitic shells of the earth's crust are remelted by the rise of heat accumulated at still greater depths and derived from the decomposition of radio-active elements. In this way basic and acid magmas become available for intrusion. Magmas of intermediate composition are produced by the inter-mixture of the two extreme magmas. Holmes does not, however, exclude differentiation by crystal-sorting as a factor in producing different magmas. L. R. Wager also derives Tertiary acid magma from sial (1956).

To judge from the superficial extent of the acid and basic intrusive rocks, it would seem that the acid rocks are in excess. If, however, the basalt lavas are included in an estimate of total volumes, the volume of the basic rocks must be much the greater of the two. Figures to show the relative areas in square miles of the dominant acid and basic intrusive rocks are given in the following table. Dykes and other minor intrusions, excepting cone-sheets, are omitted. Details concerning the plutonic districts of the north of Ireland are also included.

AREAS OF PLUTONIC ROCKS IN SQUARE MILES

	GABBRO AND DOLERITE	GRANOPHYRE AND GRANITE	OTHER PLUTONIC ROCKS
Skye	$28\frac{1}{4}$	$30\frac{1}{2}$	$\frac{3}{4}$*
Rum	$3\frac{3}{4}$	$6\frac{1}{4}$	10*
St. Kilda Islands	3	1	—
Ardnamurchan	$23\frac{1}{2}$	$\frac{1}{4}$	$\frac{3}{4}$†
Mull	33	25	—
Arran	$\frac{1}{2}$	48	—
Slieve Gullion	6	22	—
Carlingford	$6\frac{1}{4}$	$11\frac{1}{4}$	—
Mourne Mountains	—	55	—
TOTALS	$104\frac{1}{4}$	$199\frac{3}{4}$	$11\frac{1}{4}$

* Ultrabasic: † Tonalite.

REFERENCES

1895. A. McHenry. On the Age of the Trachytic Rocks of Antrim. *Geol. Mag.*, dec. iv, vol. ii, pp. 260–264.

1904. A. Harker. The Tertiary Igneous Rocks of Skye. *Mem. Geol. Surv.*

1924. E. B. Bailey and others. The Tertiary and Post-Tertiary Geology of Mull, Loch Aline and Oban. *Mem. Geol. Surv.*

1928. N. L. Bowen. *The Evolution of the Igneous Rocks.* Princeton and Oxford.

1930. J. E. Richey, H. H. Thomas and others. The Geology of Ardnamurchan, North-west Mull and Coll. *Mem. Geol. Surv.*

1931. A. Holmes. The Problem of the Association of Acid and Basic Rocks in Central Complexes. *Geol. Mag.*, vol. lxviii, pp. 241–255.

1932. J. E. Richey. Tertiary Ring Structures in Britain. *Trans. Geol. Soc. Glasgow*, vol. xix, pt. i, pp. 42–140.

1933. W. Q. Kennedy. Trends of Differentiation in Basaltic Magmas. *Amer. Journ. Sci.*, vol. xxv, pp. 239–256.

1933a. J. E. Richey. Summary of the Geology of Ardnamurchan. *Proc. Geol. Assoc.*, vol. xliv, pt. 1, pp. 1–56.

1936. A. Holmes. The Idea of Contrasted Differentiation. *Geol. Mag.*, vol. lxxiii, pp. 228–238.

1936a E. M. Anderson. Dynamics of Formation of Cone-Sheets, Ring-Dykes and Cauldron-Subsidences. *Proc. Roy. Soc. Edin.*, vol. lvi, pp. 128–157.

1937. E. M. Anderson. Cone-Sheets and Ring-Dykes: the Dynamical Explanation. *Bull. Volcanol.*, sér. ii, tome i, pp. 35–40.

1937a. R. W. van Bemmelen. The Cause and Mechanism of Igneous Intrusion: with some Scottish Examples. *Trans. Geol. Soc. Glasgow*, vol. xix, pt. iii, pp. 453–492.

1937b. J. E. Richey. Some features of Tertiary Volcanicity in Scotland and Ireland. *Bull. Volcanol.*, sér. ii, tome i, pp. 13–34.

1937c. Ph. H. Kuenen. Intrusion of Cone-Sheets. *Geol. Mag.*, vol. lxxiv, pp. 177–183.

1938. W. Q. Kennedy and E. M. Anderson. Crustal Layers and the Origin of Magmas. *Bull. Volcanol.*, sér. ii, tome iii, pp. 23–41.

1938a. E. M. Anderson. The Dynamics of Sheet Intrusion. *Proc. Roy. Soc. Edin.*, vol. lviii, pp. 242–251.

1940. J. E. Richey. Association of Explosive Brecciation and Plutonic Intrusion in the British Tertiary Igneous Province. *Bull. Volcanol.*, sér. ii, tome vi, pp. 157–175.

1948. M. K. Wells and A. K. Wells. On Magma-Types and their Nomenclature. *Geol. Mag.*, vol. lxxxv, pp. 349–357.

1949. A. Holmes. The Term " Magma-Type ". *Geol. Mag.*, vol. lxxxvi, pp. 71–72.

1949a. S. I. Tomkeieff. The Term " Magma-Type ". *Geol. Mag.*, vol. lxxxvi, p. 130.

1950. C. E. Tilley. Some Aspects of Magmatic Evolution. *Quart. Journ. Geol. Soc.* vol. cvi, pp. 37–61.

1954. D. L. Reynolds. Fluidization as a Geological Process, and its Bearing on the Problem of Intrusive Granites. *Amer. Journ. Sci.*, vol. 252, pp. 577–613.

1956. L. R. Wager. A Chemical Definition of Fractionation Stages as a basis for comparison of Hawaiian, Hebridean and other Basic lavas *Geochimica et Cosmochimica Acta*, vol. 9, pp. 217–248.

1960. L. R. Wager and others. Types of Igneous Cumulates. *Journ. Petrology*, vol. i. pp. 73–85.

1963. G. M. Brown. Melting Relations of Tertiary Granitic Rocks in Skye and Rhum. *Mineralogical Mag.*, vol. 33, pp. 533–562.

2. ISLAND OF MULL

The greatest complexity marks that portion of Mull where intrusive igneous activity was mainly concentrated (1924)*. The area concerned includes the central and south-eastern parts of the island, and extends westwards to beyond Ben More, the highest mountain of the many peaks and ridges carved out of the tangle of igneous rocks. Yet it is not difficult to appreciate the main sequence of events. The earliest intrusive rocks are arranged around the old basaltic caldera (p. 47), the limits of which are defined not only by the restriction of pillow lavas to it, but also by later plutonic masses that were intruded along its margin. Next, the area of intrusion was extended towards the north-west, and igneous activity became concentrated around Beinn Chaisgidle, a mountain situated in the north-western part of the early caldera. Finally, the centre of intrusion shifted still farther to the north-west, and around Loch Bà a later caldera was formed and the youngest intrusions were emplaced. The intrusive complex of Central Mull, in fact, possesses an axis of symmetry, along which the area of activity shifted as time went on, from south-east to north-west. In addition, a focus for intrusion was situated to the west, where, around Loch Scridain and northwards to beyond Ben More, a distinctive assemblage of sheets and sills is encountered.

Within the greater part of this area the rocks are affected by a widespread kind of alteration (pneumatolysis), which was caused mainly by water-vapours derived from the numberless intrusions or from more deep-seated sources. The effects are most apparent in the case of the fine-textured basalt lavas. In these, within a circular area 16 miles in diameter, no fresh olivine is found, and veins of epidote are usually plentiful (Plate III). The emission of vapours continued until after the close of the intrusive period, for even the latest of the basic dykes are altered.

(*a*) **Intrusions around the Early Caldera.** After the eruption of the basalt lavas, plutonic masses were intruded around the margin of the early caldera, and the earlier of these pressed outwards the country rocks into a concentric series of folds (Fig. 26). Cone-sheets were also injected in immense numbers, and volcanic vents broke through at two different periods. The sequence of events is complicated, but the various assemblages of rocks can be referred simply to two successive basic—acid magmatic cycles, with a final recurrence of basic magma. This time-sequence, which is set out below, includes the basalt lavas, since these correspond to the first appearance of basic magma.

TIME-SEQUENCE FOR EARLY CALDERA

I. Basic magma:
   (i) Plateau Group of basalt lavas.
   (ii) Central Group of basalt lavas, with pillow lavas within caldera.
II. Acid magma:
   (iii) Early Granophyres of Glas Bheinn and Derrynaculen, intruded around the caldera-margin and accompanied by concentric folding.
   (iv) Explosion-vents, drilled through the early granophyres and older rocks.
   (v) Early Acid and Composite Cone-sheets, in part contemporaneous with (vi) and with the Loch Uisg Granophyre and Gabbro.

* Dates within brackets refer to References on p. 75

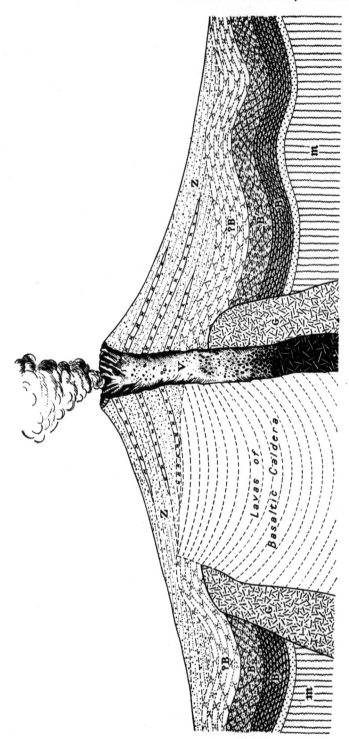

FIG. 26. *Reconstruction of the Mull Volcano, in Section, during the Early Acid Explosive Phase*

m = Moine Schists, overlain by Mesozoic strata; B, B′, ?B = Tertiary lavas of the Mull basaltic volcano: B = Plateau Group, B′ = Central Group, ?B = supposed lavas later than B′ (removed by denudation); G = Granophyre intruded around the basaltic caldera, giving rise to peripheral folding; V = Early explosion-vent, due to an acid (rhyolitic) magma; Z = Supposed ashes and rhyolitic lavas of cone-volcano (removed by denudation)

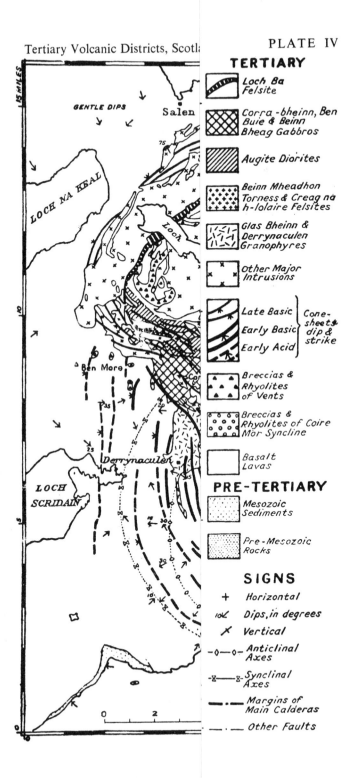

PLATE IV

Tertiary Volcanic Districts, Scotl...

TERTIARY

- Loch Ba Felsite
- Corra-bheinn, Ben Buie & Beinn Bheag Gabbros
- Augite Diorites
- Beinn Mheadhon Torness & Creag na h-Iolaire Felsites
- Glas Bheinn & Derrynaculen Granophyres
- Other Major Intrusions
- Late Basic | Cone-sheet
- Early Basic | dip &
- Early Acid | strike
- Breccias & Rhyolites of Vents
- Breccias & Rhyolites of Coire Mòr Syncline
- Basalt Lavas

PRE-TERTIARY

- Mesozoic Sediments
- Pre-Mesozoic Rocks

SIGNS

- $+$ Horizontal
- $10\angle$ Dips, in degrees
- $\times$ Vertical
- $-0-0-$ Anticlinal Axes
- $-g-g-$ Synclinal Axes
- $-\cdot-\cdot-$ Margins of Main Calderas
- $-\cdot-\cdot$ Other Faults

GENTLE DIPS

Salen

LOCH NA KEAL

Loch

△ Ben More

Derrynaculen

LOCH SCRIDAIN

Cor

0   2

III. Basic magma:
    (vi) Early Basic Cone-sheets.
    (vii) Olivine-gabbros of Ben Buie and Beinn Bheag, intruded respectively around and within the caldera-margin.

IV. Acid magma:
    (viii) Explosion-vents drilled through the gabbros and older rocks.
    (ix) Second suite of Early Acid Cone-sheets.

V. Basic magma:
    (x) Second suite of Early Basic Cone-sheets.
    (xi) Olivine-gabbro of Corra-bheinn.

This long succession perhaps resolves itself into a simpler form when followed upon the geological map (Plate IV). The augite-granophyres of Glas Bheinn and Derrynaculen, respectively to the south-east and west of the early caldera, are separated by early explosion-vents cut by cone-sheets, and by the Ben Buie gabbro. The vents contain abundant fragments of granophyre, and therefore the two granophyre masses may have originally been continuous with one another. The concentric series of folds consists of anticlines and synclines, which extend around the exterior parts of the area surrounding the early caldera. The dips of the Mesozoic sediments and basalt lavas in these folds average about 25 degrees, but in the steep Loch Don anticline to the east the beds are sometimes vertical (Fig. 27). The folds are traversed by, and earlier than, acid and basic cone-sheets belonging to the early set. Their time-relations to the earlier explosion-vents, however, are not quite clear. The vents are certainly later than the early granophyre. But, to the east, one of the peripheral synclines (Coire Mòr) appears to be filled with volcanic breccias and agglomerates, as though the folding and the eruption of the agglomerates were to be assigned to about the same time. On the other hand, the fragmentary rocks are not bedded, and are similar to breccias in the vents, and it is perhaps

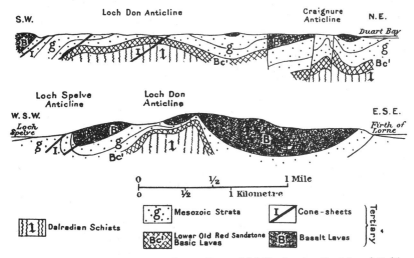

FIG. 27. *Sections across South-east Part of Mull, showing Peripheral Folds*
[Redrawn from part of Fig. 25, *Tertiary Mull Memoir*, 1924]

simpler to suppose that a vent broke through the Coire Mòr syncline, and, as now exposed, approximates closely, if not exactly, to the syncline.

The most extensive vents belong to the earlier suite. Examples are the Sgurr

Dearg and other vents extending along the eastern side of the early caldera. A large mass of these earlier vent-breccias, cut by early basic and acid cone-sheets, occurs on the south-western slopes of Ben Buie, and is earlier than the Ben Buie gabbro (Fig. 28). In addition to abundant fragments of earlier rocks, the vents contain masses and fragments of rhyolite, which represent the magma responsible for the stupendous explosive energy expended in the formation of the vents.

The succeeding early acid cone-sheets are composed of granophyre, craignurite or felsite, and are often composite, with basic selvedges usually of olivine-tholeiite. They are less numerous than the accompanying early basic cone-sheets. The latter consist of olivine-dolerite, and are similar in chemical composition to the olivine-basalt lavas of Plateau type. Individual sheets are 30 to 40 ft. in width, and their combined total thickness is estimated at one point, on Creach Bheinn, to be 3,000 ft. Altogether about a thousand individual intrusions are involved. Their angle of inclination is, on an average, 45 degrees. The belt of the early cone-sheets may have completely surrounded the early caldera, but it is now interrupted to the north-west by the intrusions of the late caldera.

The Ben Buie gabbro, the largest gabbro-mass in Mull, is intruded around the south-western side of the early caldera; it has recently been suggested that the intrusion is chonolithic in form (1959). The gabbro is brecciated along its inner side, yielding fragments to later vents (Fig. 28). It is not always possible to separate the later from the earlier vents, but the earlier vents were certainly much more extensive than the others. The Ben Bheag gabbro, on the north side of the early caldera, also serves to demonstrate the occurrence of vents of different ages. Its relation to the early cone-sheets is not known, but it may be of the same age as the Ben Buie mass.

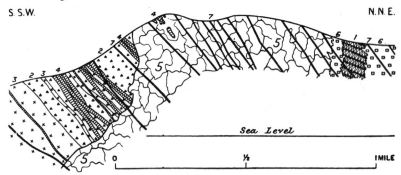

FIG. 28. *Section across Ben Buie, showing Relation of Gabbro to Vents and Cone-sheets*
1, Basalt lavas with pillow-structure; 2, early vent-agglomerates; 3, early acid cone-sheets; 4, pre-gabbro early basic cone-sheets; 5, Ben Buie gabbro; 6, post-gabbro vent-agglomerates; 7, post-gabbro early basic cone-sheets and late basic cone-sheets
[Rep. from *Tertiary Mull Memoir*, 1924, Fig. 38]

A second suite of early acid and early basic cone-sheets, the latter composed of dolerite with porphyritic feldspar, traverse the Ben Buie gabbro and the later vents (Fig. 28). They run north-westwards to terminate against the Corra-bheinn gabbro, near to which they are contact-altered. Together with the Corra-bheinn gabbro they demonstrate an extension of the area of activity to the north-west beyond the early caldera. At or about this time the area of intrusion may have been still further enlarged. Two elongate masses of augite-diorite are arranged, one on either side of Loch Ba, as though they were related to this latest centre of all. As a matter of fact, they are of comparatively early date, for they are cut by typical examples of early basic cone-sheets, and they may even antedate the Ben Buie gabbro.

Certain other masses remain to be mentioned. The extensive Loch Uisg granophyre and gabbro is a composite mass, with the gabbro occurring beneath the granophyre. It has an approximately flat roof. It cuts and is cut by early cone-sheets and evidently belongs to this early period. The large felsite masses of Beinn Mheadhon, Torness and Creag na h'Iolaire are also of early date. The two last-mentioned intrusions are cut to pieces by the early cone-sheets and other sheets. The Torness felsite is highly shattered by vent-explosions and would appear to be earlier than one of the earlier vents occurring on Sgurr Dearg. This vent is cut by the Beinn Mheadhon felsite, which is less obscured by cone-sheets than the other felsites and is seen to be a flatly undulating sheet or laccolith.

(b) **Intrusions around Beinn Chaisgidle (Centre 1) and Loch Bà (Centre 2).** The centre of intrusion first shifted north-westwards to Beinn Chaisgidle and

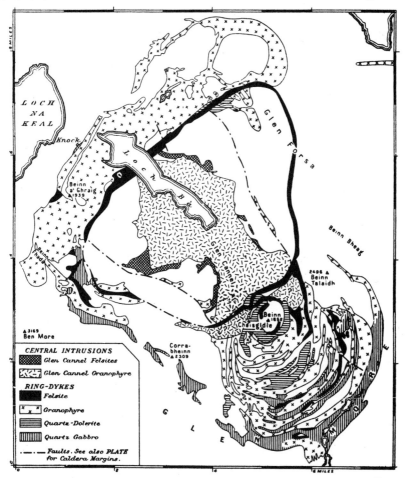

FIG. 29. *Map of Ring-dykes and Central Intrusions, Centres 1 and 2, Mull*
[Rep. from *Tertiary Mull Memoir*, 1924, Plate VI]

then to Loch Ba, around which a marked caldera of subsidence was formed at a late stage (Fig. 29). The sequence of intrusions is as follows:

Centre 1:
   (i) Ring-dykes around Beinn Chaisgidle. Several at least were intruded intermittently in the middle of the period of the late basic cone-sheets.

Centres 1 *and* 2:
   (ii) Late basic cone-sheets, mainly quartz-dolerite with columnar augite (Talaidh type), with variolites on Cruachan Dearg.

Centre 2:
   (iii) Granophyre of Glencannel, a stock-like mass with a domed roof, locally cut by many late basic cone-sheets conforming to Centre 2.
   (iv) Granophyre ring-dykes of Knock and Beinn a' Ghràig.
   (v) Felsite ring-dyke of Loch Bà, intruded along the fault-margin of the later caldera.

In addition, there are explosion-vents and associated lavas, and small masses of gabbro and dolerite, within the area of the late caldera. The exact place of these in the Mull time-sequence cannot be determined.

(i) *Ring-dykes around Beinn Chaisgidle* (*Centre* 1). A large number of ring-dykes concentrated within a small area is a description that perhaps best epitomizes the Beinn Chaisgidle complex (Fig. 29). There are about twenty distinct intrusions, with an average width of 175 yards. The rock-types concerned are quartz-gabbro, quartz-dolerite, granophyre and felsite. There are several points of interest: the occurrence of intrusions that indicate the gravitational differentiation of granophyre from quartz-gabbro; the prevalence of ' screens ' of older rocks separating adjoining ring-dykes; and the evidence of the alternating intrusion of ring-dykes and cone-sheets.

There are five excellent localities in Mull where an upward passage of quartz-gabbro into granophyre can be observed on steep hillsides. Two are situated on the Glen More ring-dyke, the outermost intrusion of the Beinn Chaisgidle suite. A description of one of these may be taken as typifying the phenomenon. A branch of the Glen More intrusion extends for a vertical distance of 1,500 ft. up the steep south-eastern slope of Cruach Choireadail, towards the western end of Glen More. Olivine-bearing quartz-gabbro at the base of the hill passes gradually upwards through various intermediate (dioritic) rocks into granophyre. A variation diagram constructed from chemical analyses of these rocks shows that there is a linear variation of the chemical constituents. In fact, the intermediate (dioritic) types correspond to simple mixtures of the two extreme types, quartz-gabbro and granophyre. The vertical variation in composition, the form of the various intrusions concerned and the petrographical characters of the intermediate rocks rule out admixture of two magmas, and it seems clear that gravitational differentiation has taken place *in situ*. According to the original account the acid fraction made its way upwards during a marked pause in crystallization that followed the separation of the gabbroic constituents (1924). After rejecting a suggestion that gravitational crystallization-differentiation may not have been involved (1936), the latest investigators advocate the operation of gravitational differentiation without any pause in crystallization (1938).

The Glen More intrusion continues north-westwards from the western end of the glen in a number of disconnected portions (Fig. 29). This limb of the ring-dyke extends north-westwards into the Loch Bà area, as though the Loch Bà centre had begun to exert an influence. The time relations of this and other

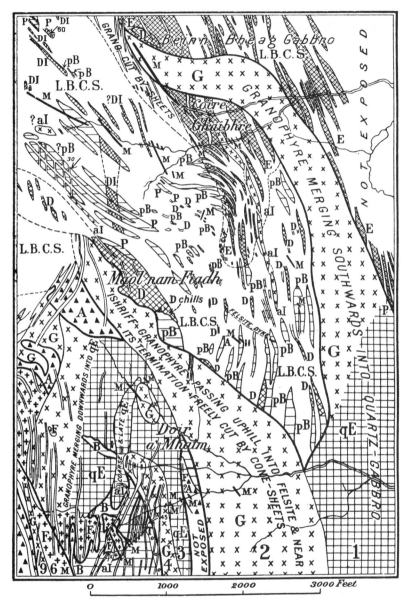

FIG. 30. *Map of Area South of Beinn Bheag, Central Mull*

1, Glen More ring-dyke; 2, Ishriff ring-dyke; 3, 4, 6, 9, other ring-dykes.
Dykes: M, basalt.
Cone-sheets: DI, dolerite; aI, acid; L.B.C.S., late basic cone-sheets (shown without ornament).
Ring-dykes: F, felsite; G, granophyre, qE, quartz-gabbro.
Screens: A, agglomerate; B, compact basalt lava; pB, porphyritic basalt lava; P, pillow-lava;
    D, dolerite; E, gabbro; also many of the cone-sheets.
[Rep. from *Tertiary Mull Memoir*, 1924, Fig. 53]

ring-dykes around Beinn Chaisgidle to one another can only be determined in a few instances, in which granophyre intrusions are found to be later than others of quartz-gabbro. As a rule, the ring-dykes are separated from one another by ' screens ' of older rocks. Two ring-dykes (Glen More and Ishriff), however, can be dated with reference to the late basic cone-sheets. At its north-eastern termination, composed of granophyre, the Glen More intrusion cuts very many cone-sheets (Fig. 30). The adjoining Ishriff granophyre also traverses the cone-sheet belt, except at its north-eastern extremity, which is cut to pieces by cone-sheets. Along its south-western series of outcrops the Glen More intrusion traverses the cone-sheet belt, but here it also becomes cut by cone-sheets towards the north-west. These two ring-dykes, therefore, were intruded during the period of the late basic cone-sheets.

(ii) *Late Basic Cone-sheets, Centres 1 and* 3. The evidence just stated indicates that the period of late basic cone-sheets was punctuated by the intrusion of ring-dykes. The arrangement of the sheets also shows that they may be sub-divided into different age-groups.

Earlier sheets conform to both centres, while later ones belong solely to the Loch Bà centre (Plate IV). They are individually only 10 to 15 ft. in width but occur in great numbers. In the Gaodhail river, west of Beinn Talaidh, the average ratio of cone-sheets to older rock is two to one (Fig. 31). The section shows 1,000 ft. of sheets, and the complete thickness of the belt is at least double this amount.

(iii) and (iv) *Granophyres of Centre* 2. The oldest of these large masses is the centrally-situated Glencannel granophyre, which is exposed beneath a slightly dome-shaped roof to a depth of 1,000 ft. The rocks forming the roof include intrusive felsite, perhaps an early, quickly cooled injection of the acid magma, basalt lavas of the Central Group, vent-agglomerates, etc. The mass may be either a stock, as shown in Fig. 32, or a thick sheet, the floor of which is not exposed, connected marginally with a ring-dyke. It is tempting to suppose that the Beinn a' Ghràig ring-dyke of granophyre, situated to the north-west just outside the faulted margin of the late caldera, represents the feeder. As already stated, however, the two granophyres are of different ages relatively to the late basic cone-sheets (p. 68).

The Beinn a' Ghràig granophyre is seen in contact with walls composed of basalt lavas for a vertical distance of nearly 2,000 ft., and ends upwards beneath a roof of lavas. The lavas are lying practically horizontally, and the intrusion affords an excellent example of the replacement of bedded rocks by a broad ring-dyke. It is supposed that a great elongate block of lavas was separated off by two parallel ring-dyke fractures united by a cross roof-fracture, and that the block subsided into the rising granophyre magma, which thus occupied the space left.

The less massive Knock granophyre extends along the outer side of the Beinn a' Ghràig ring-dyke, from which it is separated by a narrow ' screen ' of basalt lavas. The ' screen ' is seen on the eastern side of Beinn a' Ghràig to extend from the base almost to the summit of this steep-sided mountain, 2,000 ft. in height. It is continuous with one of the cappings of lava that form part of the roof of the Beinn a' Ghràig granophyre (Figs. 29, 32).

In composition the three granophyres of Centre 2 differ slightly from one another. The rocks composing the Glencannel and Beinn a' Ghràig masses are closely similar, both containing a green pleochroic augite. Radiate and spheru-litic structures, however, appear to be specially prevalent in the Glencannel

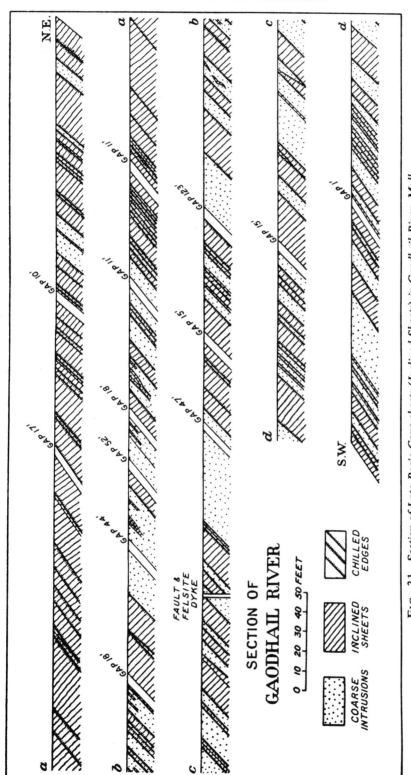

FIG. 31. *Section of Late Basic Cone-sheets (Inclined Sheets) in Gaodhail River, Mull* [Rep., with slight alteration, from 'Summary of Progress' for 1910 (*Mem. Geol. Surv.*), 1911, p. 36]

granophyre. The Knock intrusion is distinguished from the others by the occurrence of a brownish augite, and by its comparative richness in plagioclase feldspar.

(v) *Late Caldera and Loch Bà Felsite Ring-dyke.* The late caldera around Loch Bà is bounded by a complete ring-fault along which a ring-dyke of felsite extends almost continuously (Fig. 29). The felsite is later than the fault-brecciation. The fault and ring-dyke are observed in a few places to be inclined outwards from Centre 2 at angles of 70 to 80 degrees (Fig. 32). The great block enclosed by it can be shown to have subsided relatively to the surrounding rocks for a vertical distance of at least 3,000 ft.; for, where the fault and ring-dyke cross Loch Bà, the basalt lavas within the fault belong to the Central Group of Mull, whereas the lavas outside the fault at the level of the loch are about 3,000 ft. below the top of the Plateau Group, as developed in this neighbourhood. The felsite ring-dyke is later than the granophyres of Centre 2, and is not cut by any intrusions excepting north-west basic dykes. It is the latest ring intrusion of Mull. It is, however, brecciated by explosion where it crosses a stream west of Beinn Chaisgidle, and it is possible that it extended upwards to surround a surface-caldera from which lavas and ashes were erupted.

(c) **Andesitic Sills of Loch Scridain.** These sills, and sheets, are mostly of similar rock-types and are congregated within a strictly limited area (Fig. 33). They are irregular intrusions and vary both in direction and in the amount of their inclination, except in the neighbourhood of Ben More, where the majority of the sheets dip to the west or north-west fairly constantly. In this district,

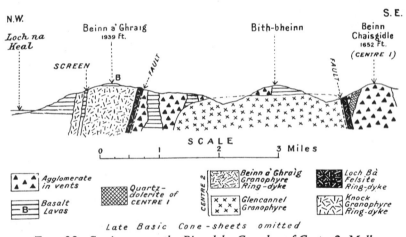

FIG. 32. *Section across the Ring-dyke Complex of Centre 2, Mull*

tholeiite is the chief rock-type, but elsewhere andesites (inninmorite and leidleite) are prevalent. Glassy and stony varieties of these two types of andesite are frequently associated in the same intrusive mass, in which 'cores' of glassy pitchstone are surrounded by stony 'sheaths'. The only difference, chemically, between the two rock-varieties is that the pitchstone contains a notable amount of combined water. The 'sheath and core' structure is explained by supposing that the magma consolidated as pitchstone in the first instance and that during later stages of cooling the outer parts, or those bordering joints, were able to get rid of the dissolved water and became devitrified (1917).

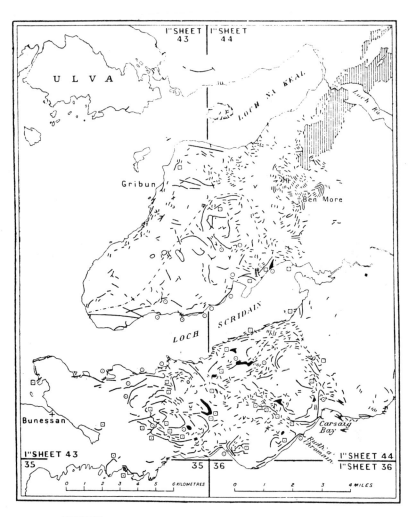

Knock and Beinn a' Ghràig Granophyres.

Sills and sheets of Loch Scridain suite.

Northern limit of pitchstones and xenoliths.

⊙ ' Accidental ' xenoliths containing sapphire.

□ Other ' accidental ' xenoliths.

FIG. 33. *Map showing Distribution of Sills of Loch Scridain Suite, S.W. Mull*
[Rep. from *Tertiary Mull Memoir*, 1924, Fig. 42]

F

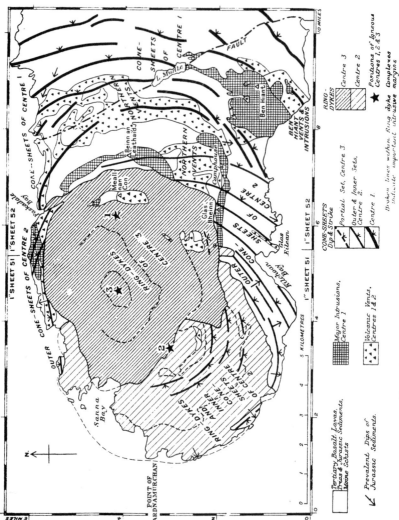

FIG. 34. *Map of Ring Complexes of Ardnamurchan*

[Rep. from 'The Geology of Ardnamurchan,' etc. (*Mem. Geo. Surv.*), 1930, Plate II]

The Loch Scridain sills are still more remarkable for their xenolithic inclusions. Accidental xenoliths, composed of various sedimentary and igneous rocks, are abundant. Many of these are of altered clay-rock, now in the form of glass, or buchite. This rock often contains conspicuous crystals of sapphire (1922). Another interesting mineral is mullite, a silicate of alumina closely resembling sillimanite but differing in its chemical formula (1924a). Other characteristic minerals are cordierite and anorthite. Reactions have taken place between the xenoliths and the magma, and these show that slow cooling proceeded from about 1,400°C to 1,200°C, presumably in a magma-reservoir, and that thereafter rapid cooling followed when the magma was intruded.

The date of the Loch Scridain sills can not be definitely fixed, but, to judge from their composition, it seems probable that they are contemporaneous with part of the late basic cone-sheet cycle of Central Mull.

REFERENCES

1917. E. M. ANDERSON and E. G. RADLEY. The Pitchstones of Mull and their Genesis. *Quart. Journ. Geol. Soc.*, vol. lxxi for 1915, pp. 205–216.

1922. H. H. THOMAS. On certain Xenolithic Tertiary Minor Intrusions in the Island of Mull (Argyllshire). *Quart. Journ. Geol. Soc.*, vol. lxxviii, pp. 229–259.

1924. E. B. BAILEY and others. The Tertiary and Post-Tertiary Geology of Mull, Loch Aline and Oban. *Mem. Geol. Surv.*

1924a. N. L. BOWEN, J. W. GREIG and E. G. ZIES. Mullite, a silicate of Alumina. *Journ. Wash. Acad. Sci.*, vol. xiv, pp. 183–191.

1925. E. B. BAILEY and E. M. ANDERSON. The Geology of Staffa, Iona and Western Mull. *Mem. Geol. Surv.*

1930. J. E. RICHEY, H. H. THOMAS and others. The Geology of Ardnamurchan, North-west Mull and Coll. *Mem. Geol. Surv.*

1931. A. G. MACGREGOR. Scottish Pyroxene–granulite Hornfelses and Odenwald Beerbachites. *Geol. Mag.*, vol. lxviii, pp. 506–521.

1936. A. HOLMES. The Idea of Contrasted Differentiation. *Geol. Mag.*, vol. lxxiii, pp. 228–238.

1938. C. KOOMANS and P. H. KUENEN. On the Differentiation of the Glen More Ring-Dyke, Mull. *Geol. Mag.*, vol. lxxv, pp. 145–160.

1948. E. B. BAILEY and J. E. RICHEY. Mull and Ardnamurchan. *Internat. Geol. Congress, 18th Session, Gt. Brit.* 1948. *Guide to Excursion A*12, pp. 2–12.

1958. D. S. BUIST. The Bostonite of Rudh' a' Chromain, Carsaig, Mull. *Geol. Mag.*, vol. xcv, pp. 463–464.

1959. W. M. LOBJOIT. On the Form and Mode of Emplacement of the Ben Buie Intrusion, Island of Mull, Argyllshire. *Geol. Mag.*, vol. xcvi, pp. 393–402.

3. ARDNAMURCHAN

The western portion of the peninsula of Ardnamurchan is composed largely of Tertiary volcanic vents, ring-dykes and cone-sheets, which are arranged in concentric series around three centres of intrusion (pp. 55, 76). The sea has made considerable inroads upon the complex, and around the nose of the peninsula has cut inwards as far as a centrally situated massif of gabbro. There is, however, ample evidence of prolonged igneous extrusion and intrusion, and the district serves perhaps better than any other to illustrate the salient features of Tertiary igneous activity (1930)*. It is less complicated than Mull, and smaller in size, and is easily accessible to visitors.

There is no direct evidence that a central volcano existed in Ardnamurchan during the basaltic phase, when the plateau lavas were erupted. The local igneous history begins with the formation of explosion-vents that are seen to pierce the small outcrops of plateau lavas remaining and the more extensive Mesozoic sediments and Moine Schists (Plate VII). The vents occupy a large area to the east of the gabbro-massif, which is of later date (Fig. 34). They were originally still more extensive, for masses of agglomerate similar to those infilling them are involved in the eastern half of the gabbro-area. A few major intrusions and numbers of cone-sheets are associated with the vents, and from their arrangement it is clear that an early Centre of Intrusion (1) was situated near the eastern margin of the gabbro.

The mapping of the gabbro-massif disclosed the fact that it consists of a number of ring-dykes which extend around two later centres. The second centre (2) lies to the west, and around it cone-sheets, in two suites, and a single elongate vent are also arranged. Like the vent-complex of Centre 1, this second congeries of intrusions is in large part replaced by masses related to the latest centre (3), which is located almost midway between the two earlier centres. Around it, ring-dykes were intruded, together with a few cone-sheets. There are no volcanic vents, and few signs of brecciation by explosive gases, though in the case of several ring-dykes of Centre 2 there is frequent evidence of this. It would seem as if we are observing in Ardnamurchan the roots of volcanoes cut at different crustal levels. An ever-growing volcanic pile would appear to have risen above the crustal level which erosion has now exposed. Looked at in the broadest way, the complex may be regarded as a volcanic vent (represented by the vent-complex of Centre 1) pierced by two successive plugs (the ring-dykes complexes of Centres 2 and 3), with fringes of outwardly spreading sheets (cone-sheets) intruded at various times.

The time-sequence is, briefly, as follows (Fig. 34):

Centre 1 { Volcanic vents, mainly filled with agglomerates, are traversed by massive cone-sheets and by major intrusions, in part sheet-like, in part dyke-like or plug-like in form.

Centre 2 { Abundant cone-sheets, constituting an outer set, surround a succeeding complex of ring-dykes, mainly composed of gabbro. The latter fall into two age-groups, respectively earlier and later than an inner set of cone-sheets. An elongate vent at Glas Eilean, near Kilchoan, is later than the outer cone-sheets.

Centre 3 { A suite of ring-dykes of gabbroic rock-types surrounds more acid masses (tonalite and quartz-monzonite). The outermost and probably oldest ring-dyke is cut by a few cone-sheets.

In addition, there are numbers of linear dykes, mainly trending north-west. Some are composed of acid rocks, but the majority are of basic types. They are of various ages. Many dykes, traversing the ring-dykes, are the latest intrusions of the district.

(a) **Ring Complex of Centre 1.** Since the vents are so extensive, it seems probable that a number of orifices of different ages are involved. The best examples are exposed on Ben Hiant, where there is a complicated area of vents and associated intrusions lying outside the boundary of the main group of vents

* Dates within brackets refer to References on p. 86.

A. AGGLOMERATE CLIFFS OF MACLEAN'S NOSE
(For explanation, *see* p. 77)
[Rep. from 'The Geology of Ardnamurchan', etc. (*Mem. Geol. Surv.*), 1930, Pl. III]

B. COLUMNAR PITCHSTONE LAVA
(For explanation, *see* p. 77)
[Rep. from 'Guide to the Geological Model of Ardnamurchan' (*Mem. Geol. Surv.*), 1934, Pl. IV B]

MATERIALS FILLING SOUTH-WEST VENT OF BEN HIANT, ARDNAMURCHAN

situated farther north. Perhaps the Ben Hiant vents are the earliest of all. There is evidence that they possessed wide craters with walls at least 1,000 ft. in height. These great explosion-cavities were filled in layer by layer with agglomerates and beds of tuff, while pitchstone lavas flowed out from time to time over the rising accumulations of fragmental materials (1938). An earlier vent, to the north-east, was succeeded by a crater of still larger size to the south-west. The wall of the south-west crater has been in large part denuded away, so that agglomerate-cliffs that rise to a great height at Maclean's Nose, at the south-western end of the mountain, represent as it were the cast of the ancient crater (Plate VA). In the cliffs, beds of tuff occur at intervals of about 20 ft., and columnar pitchstone lavas are seen at two or three different levels on the adjoining hillside. Individual pitchstone lavas present the three-tier structure characteristic of the columnar basaltic flows of Staffa and elsewhere (p. 47). Fragments in the agglomerates are largely trachyte, but rhyolite is also found, together with blocks of big-feldspar basalt, sometimes of enormous size. A plug-like mass of dolerite with porphyritic feldspar is intruded against the agglomerates, and is contact-altered near a great mass of quartz-dolerite (the Ben Hiant Intrusion),

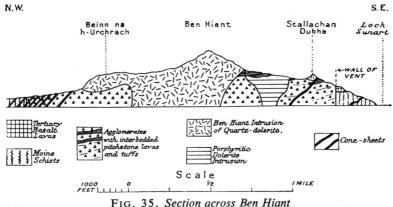

FIG. 35. *Section across Ben Hiant*
[Rep. from 'The Geology of Ardnamurchan', etc. (*Mem. Geol. Surv.*), 1930, Fig. 19]

which forms the summit of the mountain. This intrusion extends upwards from sea-level to spread out laterally as though filling some great crater (Fig. 35). On the northern slopes of Ben Hiant, however, it sends out tongues parallel to adjacent cone-sheets. In chemical composition the rock composing it is similar to that forming the cone-sheets, and the Ben Hiant Intrusion would seem to come nearer to the cone-sheets in time than to the particular vents with which it is associated.

The extensive vents along lower ground to the north of Ben Hiant, termed the Northern Vents, are less well exposed. Their materials consist largely of brecciated older rocks, but rhyolite and trachyte fragments are also prevalent, as on Ben Hiant. Large areas of basalt lavas, which have slipped down into the vents from some higher level, occur within them (1940). The Northern Vents are perhaps later than the Ben Hiant vents, because included fragments of quartz-dolerite, broken from once extensive intrusions of this rock-type, are often to be observed: such rocks are unknown from the Ben Hiant agglomerates.

Major intrusions distributed around Centre 1 consist of porphyritic dolerite, of gabbro with marginal porphyritic dolerite and of fine-grained granophyre.

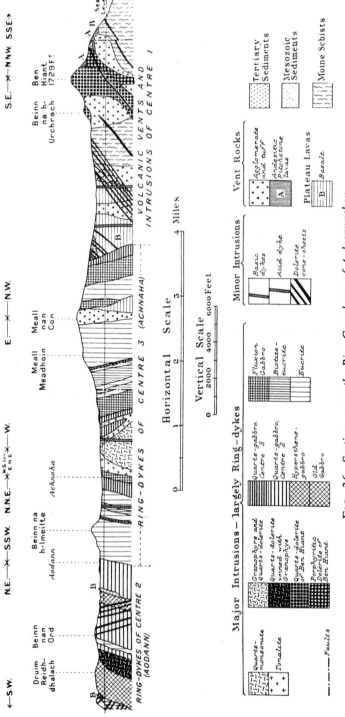

FIG. 36. *Section across the Ring Complexes of Ardnamurchan*

[Rep. from ' Guide to the Geological Model of Ardnamurchan ' (*Mem. Geol. Surv.*), 1934, Fig. 20]

The cone-sheets are more massive than those connected with the later centres. They are composed of quartz-dolerite, like the outer cone-sheets of Centre 2, which succeeded them.

(b) **Ring Complex of Centre 2.** Perhaps the most interesting features of the Ardnamurchan complex are the fact that igneous activity shifted successively from one centre to another and the extraordinary regularity in the arrangement of its intrusive rock-masses around the various centres. In the case of Centre 2 the date of the change in the position of the focus is clearly demonstrable. The earliest intrusions related to it, the numerous cone-sheets of the outer set, traverse the vents and major intrusions of Centre 1. A still earlier event in the history of Centre 2 was the formation of an elongate dome, extending east-north-eastwards towards Centre 1. The dome is indicated by the steep outward dips of the Mesozoic strata around the plutonic area (Fig. 34); and its age is ascertained from the fact that the tilted sediments are traversed by the outer cone-sheets inclined at their usual angles. The change of focus, it is to be noted, was not accompanied by an incursion of a different magma. Quartz-dolerite cone-sheets formed the last phase around Centre 1 and the first around Centre 2.

The local abundance of the outer cone-sheets is shown on Fig. 37, and it is estimated that near Kilchoan the belt consisted of a total thickness of over 3,000 ft. of sheets. They are inclined at angles of 35 to 45 degrees, and are everywhere directed downwards towards Centre 2. Though the western part of the Ardnamurchan complex is hidden beneath the sea, it seems almost certain that the outer cone-sheets completely surrounded the centre. Towards the inner side of the belt, west of Kilchoan, sheets composed of dolerite with porphyritic feldspars become plentiful, and are perhaps later than exterior sheets. At any rate, the same type of rock constitutes members of the inner set, which is of still later date, since it traverses many of the ring-dykes of Centre 2. These interior sheets, being nearer the centre, are inclined at high angles, 65 to 70 degrees. The contact-alteration and truncation of outer cone-sheets that adjoin the outermost and probably oldest ring-dyke show that the intrusion of ring-dykes next ensued.

The ring-dykes around Centre 2 are enumerated below in the order of their relative ages, so far as determinable (Fig. 38):

(a)	Hypersthene-gabbro of Ardnamurchan Point	
(b)	Old Gabbro of Lochan an Aodainn	
(c)	Quartz-gabbro of Garbh-dhail	
(c')	Granophyre of Grigadale	Earlier than Inner
(c'')	Older Quartz-gabbro of Beinn Bhuidhe	Cone-sheets
(d)	Quartz-gabbro of Aodann	
(e)	Quartz-dolerite of Sgùrr nam Meann, veined by granophyre	
(f)	Eucrite of Beinn nan Ord	
(g)	Quartz-gabbro of Loch na Caorach	Later than Inner
(h)	Younger Quartz-gabbro of Beinn Bhuidhe	Cone-sheets
(i)	Fluxion Gabbro of Portuairk	

The ring-dykes, of both Centres 2 and 3, possess individual points of interest in regard to their prevalent rock-types and local variations in composition, their marginal facies and external form, the included fragments of earlier rocks (xenoliths), and the changes imposed upon the ring-dykes after their consolidation by neighbouring intrusions, earth-movements, etc. These features, however, can only be described here in a general way.

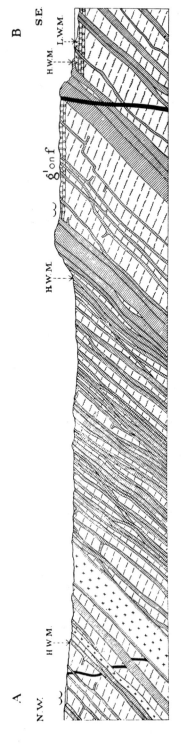

FIG. 37. *Section showing Cone-sheets along Shore South of Kilchoan, Ardnamurchan*
[Rep. from 'The Geology of Ardnamurchan', etc. (*Mem. Geol. Surv.*), 1930, Fig. 24]

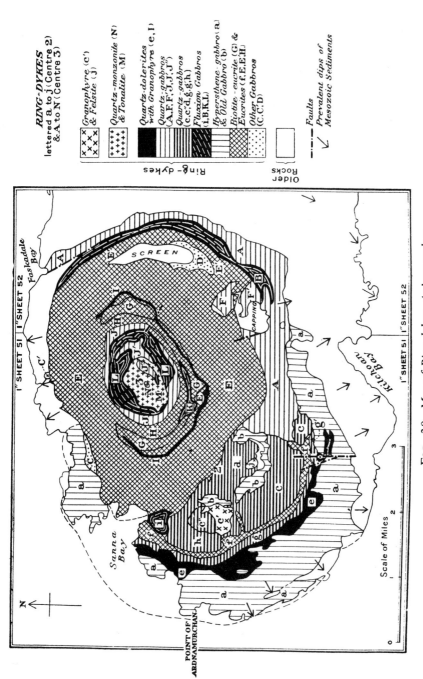

RING-DYKES
lettered a to j (Centre 2)
& A to N (Centre 3)

Granophyre (c')
& Felsite (j)

Quartz-monzonite (N)
& Tonalite (M)

Quartz-dolerites
with Granophyre (e,I)

Quartz-gabbros
(A,F,F',I,J,J')

Quartz-gabbros
(c,c',d,g,h)
Fluxion Gabbros
(I,B,K,L)

Hypersthene-gabbro (a)
& Old Gabbro (b)

Biotite-eucrite (G) &
Eucrites (f,E,E,H)

Other Gabbros
(C,C,D)

Ring-dykes

Older
Rocks

Faults

Prevalent dips of
Mesozoic Sediments

FIG. 38. *Map of Ring-dykes, Ardnamurchan*

[Rep. from 'The Geology of Ardnamurchan' etc. (*Mem. Geol. Surv.*), 1930, Plate V]

In regard to composition, it is noteworthy that each intrusion is mainly composed of a particular rock-type, but also includes variations of one sort or another. For example, the hypersthene-gabbro (*a*) consists typically of a rock with basic plagioclase feldspar, monoclinic and rhombic pyroxene, olivine and iron-ore. Locally, with olivine particularly abundant and bytownite or anorthite-feldspar dominant, there is an approach to eucrite, or, when an acid mesostasis is developed, a close similarity to quartz-gabbro. The development of distinctive marginal facies to the ring-dykes forms one of the main aids to their separation in the field. Sometimes, as in the hypersthene-gabbro (*a*), a fine-grained margin is developed, due to more rapid cooling along the contacts with older rocks.

FIG. 39. *View of the Western Side of Beinn na Seilg*

a, Hypersthene-gabbro; *c*, Quartz-gabbro of Garbh-dhail; *e*, Quartz-dolerite of Sgùrr nam Meann; *f*, Eucrite of Beinn nan Ord; *g'*, Quartz-gabbro of Beinn na Seilg. Broken lines indicate margins of ring-dykes (not shown in foreground).

NOTE—Hollows extending across the view are eroded along crush-lines.

[Rep. from ' The Geology of Ardnamurchan ', etc. (*Mem. Geol. Surv.*), 1930, Fig. 36]

There may also be a difference in composition, with somewhat more acid rocks forming a marginal fringe, or a development of banding due to flow-movement in a partially crystallized magma. According to M. K. Wells, layering or banding, although only locally well developed, is a characteristic feature of a large part of the hypersthene-gabbro; he suggests that the banding is due to crystal-precipitate accumulation (1954*b*).

Along intrusive junctions xenoliths of the older rocks are often contained in the later mass. Xenolithic igneous material is sometimes distributed throughout a ring-dyke and is often of particular interest. Fine-grained basic strips are plentiful, for example, in the hypersthene-gabbro. They look like dykes or sheets cutting the gabbro but are composed of entirely recrystallized rocks (granulites), and they are certainly inclusions. The basic granular hornfelses within the hypersthene-gabbro (1930, 1931*a*) have received much attention in recent years. It is agreed that the great majority are granulitized inclusions of igneous rocks (lavas and intrusive types) but the status of certain xenoliths alleged to be of sedimentary origin is doubtful (1951, 1954, 1954*b*). Mobilization of xenolithic igneous material has been suggested as one explanation of the intrusion, in the gabbro, of certain basic veins and narrow dykes of distinctive character (1954b).

The three-dimensional shapes of intrusions can be decided where a ring-dyke, or a number of ring-dykes, crosses a steep hillside, or, less frequently, by observing the inclination of the junction at actual contacts with older rocks. Typically the margins are very highly inclined, except of course in cases where an intrusion ends upwards beneath a roof. Sometimes it can be shown that the inclination is definitely outwards from the centre, as in the case of the Loch Bà ring-dyke of Mull (p. 72).

According to M. K. Wells the hypersthene-gabbro of Centre 2, Ardnamurchan, originally had a domed-up *roof* of Mesozoic sediments, of which there are extensive relics on the south and south-west margins between Kilchoan and Port Min, and it may not be a comparatively steep-sided ring-dyke (1954b). Wells alleges that the quartz-dolerite ring-dyke of Sgùrr nam Meann, also related to Centre 2 of Ardnamurchan, has a very irregular outer margin because of the local injection of flat-lying sill-apophyses into the adjacent hypersthene-gabbro (1954c).

Changes later than the consolidation of the rock that are caused directly by later intrusions are due to the heat or vapours derived from such masses. A characteristic effect ascribed to reheating is best developed in the Old Gabbro (*b*) which is hemmed in by younger intrusions. The rock is dead-black in colour, owing to the darkening of the basic plagioclase feldspar by myriads of dust-like, ultra-microscopic particles (1931). This 'clouding' of the feldspars is also found along the contacts of various other older masses with later intrusions. Also, an older rock may be completely or partly recrystallized. Such granulitic rocks, or granulites, are finer in texture than the original rock.

The production of vapours is especially characteristic of acid masses, of which there are few examples in Ardnamurchan. It is best seen around and within the vents of Centre 1, affecting older rocks such as the basalt lavas, in which

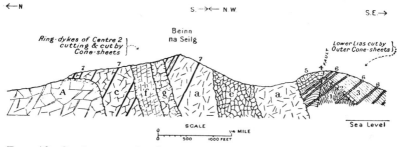

FIG. 40. *Section across South-west Part of Ardnamurchan Igneous Complex*
1, Highland Schists; 2, Trias; 3, Lias; 4, Inferior Oolite (limestone and sandstone); 5, Tertiary basalt lavas; 6, Outer cone-sheets of Centre 2; 7, Inner cone-sheets of Centre 2. Ring-dykes *a*, *c*, *e*, *f*, *g* and *A* as lettered on Fig. 38, p. 81.
[Rep. from ' The Geology of Ardnamurchan ', etc. (*Mem. Geol. Surv.*), 1930, Fig. 28]

veins of epidote are developed, the olivine is decomposed and chlorite formed from pyroxene and other minerals.

Earth movements are responsible for crushing along the outer margin of the quartz-gabbro (*c*). Linear crushes and veins of flinty crush-rock show that intense pressures were involved. It is concluded in this particular instance that, after the ring-dykes earlier than the quartz-dolerite (e) had been intruded, a new ring-dyke fracture was formed close to the outer margin of the quartz-gabbro (c) and movement and marginal crushing of the central block resulted. Along the fracture the ring-dykes (e), (f), (g) were successively intruded. The eucrite (f) affords an example of a different kind of brecciation, the result of explosive gases derived from an ascending acid magma (1930, 1940). Comminution of the rock on a minute scale was followed by the injection here and there of fine veins of granophyre and the general recrystallization of the broken crystals. Such complete brecciation, if it extended to higher levels, would undoubtedly lead to the formation of a volcanic vent. Whether this happened at any time in the history of the ring-dyke complex of Centre 2 there are, of course, no means of knowing. The elongate vent of Glas Eilean (1940, 1954a) is the only instance of its kind seen at the present level of denudation in connection with Centre 2 (cf. p. 58).

Ring-dyke (e), the quartz-dolerite of Sgùrr nam Meann, characterized by intricate net-veining by granophyre, has been studied in some detail by M. K. Wells (1954c); he infers that granophyric material was produced by differentiation during the crystallization of the dolerite and that, when the dolerite was almost consolidated but still hot, gas explosions occurred, shattered the dolerite and facilitated the intimate penetration of the brecciated rock by the granophyric residuum.

(c) **Ring Complex of Centre 3.** This complex provides as striking examples of ring-dykes as any to be found in the West of Scotland. The complex is completely preserved; and, regarded as a unit, it cuts through and replaces large portions of the two earlier ring complexes: it has not made room for itself by pushing them aside. The demonstration that there are ring complexes of different ages in Ardnamurchan is completed by the evidence afforded by Centre 3. Its outermost intrusions come into contact with many of the rocks related to the earlier centres, and are found to be of later date.

Noteworthy features which the complex presents are: (1) the slightly oval shape of the complex as a whole, which is reflected in the shapes of the individual intrusions; (2) the fact that its longer axis coincides with the line joining Centre 2 and Centre 3, the direction in which igneous activity shifted; (3) the failure of

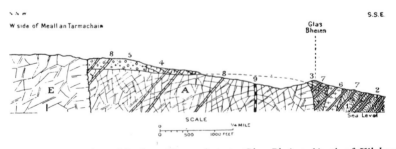

FIG. 41. *Section from Meall an Tarmachain to Glas Bheinn, North of Kilchoan*

1, Moine Schists; 2, Trias; 3, Lower Lias (limestone and shale); 4, Tertiary basalt lavas; 5, Vent-agglomerate (Centre 1); 6, Porphyritic dolerite of Glas Bheinn (Centre 1); 7, Outer cone-sheets of Centre 2; 8, Cone-sheets (Centre 3); 9, Quartz-felsite dyke; A, Quartz-gabbro ring-dyke (Centre 3); E, Great Eucrite ring-dyke (Centre 3).
[Rep. from ' The Geology of Ardnamurchan ', etc. (*Mem. Geol. Surv.*) 1930 **Fig.** 39]

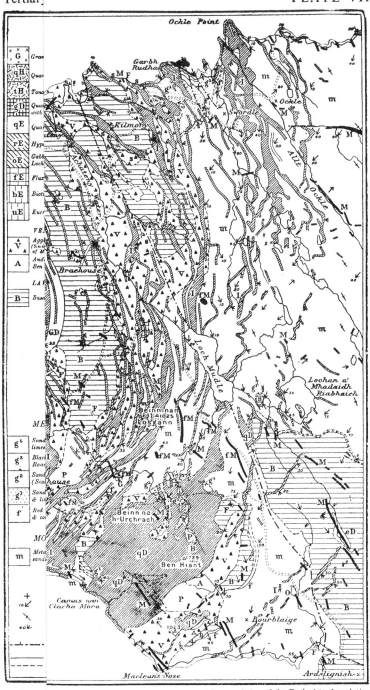

(By permission of the Geologists Association)

Surv.), 1930]

many ring-dykes to extend around the northern part of the complex; (4) the time relations of the component intrusions, in general younger ring-dykes being intruded within older ones, with the youngest masses of all at the centre of the complex. These features in part find an explanation in the accepted theory concerning the method of intrusion of ring-dykes (p. 57). It is noteworthy that the history of Centre 2 appears to have ended and that of Centre 3 to have begun with the intrusion of a similar magma (quartz-gabbro). Our knowledge is insufficient to explain fully why centres of intrusion such as those found in Ardnamurchan and Mull should shift from one point to another. But it would appear as if the phenomenon were accompanied by a lateral displacement of the magma available for intrusion (*see also* pp. 67, 79).

The ring-dykes, in the general order of age, are as follows (Fig. 38), a few small masses being omitted:

(A) Quartz-gabbro of Faskadale.
(B) Fluxion Gabbro of Allt Faskadale.
(C) Gabbro of Plocaig.
(D) Porphyritic Gabbro of Meall nan Con screen.
(E¹) Outer Eucrite.
(E) Great Eucrite.
(F) Quartz-gabbro of Meall an Tarmachain.
(G) Biotite-eucrite.
(H) Inner Eucrite.
(I)   Quartz-dolerite veined with granophyre.
(J)   Quartz-biotite-gabbro.
(K) Fluxion Biotite-gabbro of Sìthean Mòr.
(L) Fluxion Biotite-gabbro of Glendrian.
(M) Tonalite.
(N) Quartz-monzonite.

FIG. 42. *View of Contact of Great Eucrite Ring-dyke, forming Vertically Jointed Crag, with Meall nan Con ' Screen ', Ardnamurchan*
[Rep. from ' The Geology of Ardnamurchan ', etc. (*Mem. Geol. Surv.*), 1930, Fig. 41]

The outermost and oldest ring-dyke (A) is traversed on its southern side by a few centrally inclined sheets, which probably constitute a partially developed set of cone-sheets (Fig. 34). They are earlier than the Great Eucrite (E), near to which they are highly altered (granulitized).

The effects imposed upon the older rocks around the outer margin of the Great Eucrite vary much in intensity. The porphyritic gabbro (D), for example, is converted into a banded granulitized rock at the actual contact. Clouding of the feldspars is a less intense alteration affecting the quartz-gabbro (A) at a point beneath a roof of older rocks on the west side of Meall an Tarmachain. In the valley to the west, part of the same gabbro is apparently unaltered, though it is veined by and is certainly earlier than the eucrite.

The Great Eucrite is the most remarkable ring-dyke in Ardnamurchan, being a complete ring, a mile in annular width. It is composed of a durable rock and forms a conspicuous belt of high ground marked by steep slopes and crags along its inner side (Plate VI). The ring-dykes within it, constituting the Interior Complex, consist of rock-types characterized by containing biotite. The intrusions can be arranged in an order of increasing acidity, and of increasing biotite-content. Biotite-gabbros are succeeded by tonalite, and the latter by quartz-monzonite. These biotite-bearing rocks are an exceptional occurrence in the Tertiary province. They are considered to be due to a very complete intermixture, before intrusion, of acid magma with basic materials.

REFERENCES

1930. J. E. RICHEY, H. H. THOMAS and others. The Geology of Ardnamurchan, North-west Mull and Coll. *Mem. Geol. Surv.*

1931. A. G. MACGREGOR. Clouded Feldspars and Thermal Metamorphism. *Mineralogical Mag.*, vol. xxii pp. 524–538. (Ardnamurchan p. 533).

1931a. A. G. MACGREGOR. Scottish Pyroxene-granulite Hornfelses and Odenwald Beerbachites. *Geol. Mag.*, vol. lxviii pp. 506–521.

1933. J. E. RICHEY. Summary of the Geology of Ardnamurchan. *Proc. Geol. Assoc.*, vol. xliv, pt. 1, pp. 1–56. (Excursion Guide).

1938. J. E. RICHEY. The Rhythmic Eruptions of Ben Hiant, Ardnamurchan, a Tertiary Volcano. *Bull. Volcanol.*, sér. ii, tome iii, pp. 2–21.

1940. J. E. RICHEY. Association of Explosive Brecciation and Plutonic Intrusion in the British Tertiary Igneous Province. *Bull. Volcanol.*, sér. ii, tome vi, pp. 157–175.

1948. E. B. BAILEY and J. E. RICHEY. Mull and Ardnamurchan. *Inter. Geol. Congress*, 18th Session, Gt. Brit. 1948. *Guide to Excursion A*12, pp. 13–22.

1951. M. K. WELLS. Sedimentary Inclusions in the Hypersthene-gabbro, Ardnamurchan, Argyllshire. *Mineralogical Mag.*, vol. xxix, pp. 715–736.

1954. G. M. BROWN. A suggested Igneous Origin for the Banded Granular Hornfelses within the Hypersthene-gabbro of Ardnamurchan, Argyllshire. *Mineralogical Mag.*, vol. xxx, pp. 529–533.

1954a. D. L. REYNOLDS. Fluidization as a Geological Process, and its Bearing on the Problem of Intrusive Granites. *Amer. Journ. Sci.*, vol. 252, pp. 577–613. (Glas Eilean vent, p. 589).

1954b. M. K. WELLS. The Structure and Petrology of the Hypersthene-gabbro Intrusion, Ardnamurchan, Argyllshire. *Quart. Journ. Geol. Soc.*, vol. cix for 1953, pp. 367–395.

1954c. M. K. WELLS. The Structure of the Granophyric Quartz-dolerite Intrusion of Centre 2, Ardnamurchan and the Problem of Net-Veining. *Geol. Mag.*, vol. xci, pp. 293–307.

4. SKYE AND ADJACENT ISLANDS

The great mountain group of Central Skye, eroded out of Tertiary plutonic masses, presents many geological contrasts as well as resemblances to the plutonic districts of Mull and Ardnamurchan. Unlike these highly complicated areas, there is an apparent simplicity in the arrangement of its component parts. Different kinds of scenery mark the two main geological areas of which it consists. The rugged Cuillin with its cluster of serrated peaks, some twenty of which are over 3,000 ft. in height, is formed mainly of gabbro (Plate IA). It

FIG. 43. *Intrusive Junction of Quartz-gabbro of Meall an Tarmachain (left) with Outer Eucrite, South-east Side of Meall an Tarmachain*
[Rep. from ' The Geology of Ardnamurchan ', etc. (*Mem. Geol. Surv.*), 1930, Fig. 44]

lies to the west of a group of smoothly contoured mountains composed of granophyre and granite, which constitute the Red Hills. In addition, there are a number of masses of volcanic agglomerate and several suites of minor intrusions. According to A. Harker, who mapped the district for the Geological Survey, the agglomerates are mainly earlier than the plateau lavas, and the plutonic rocks are earlier than the majority of the minor intrusions (1904, 1904a, 1910)*.

* Dates within brackets refer to References on p. 94.

In the Cuillin Hills an arcuate mass of ultrabasic rock is enveloped and intruded by the gabbro. The gabbro consists of a complex of intrusions and is succeeded by the acid masses of the Red Hills. Of the minor intrusions, centrally inclined sheets (cone-sheets) and radial and tangential suites of dykes traverse the Cuillin gabbro, which is also crossed by a swarm of north-west basic dykes. Many of the north-west dykes are earlier than the cone-sheets. In and around the Red Hills there are also north-west dykes, both basic and acid in rock-type, and a group of composite sills (Fig. 44). In regard to the sequence of magmas, therefore, the order, ultrabasic, basic, acid, accounts for the plutonic phase, while the reverse of this order has been applied in a general way to explain the minor intrusions. The composite (basic-acid) sills near Broadford have been taken to mark the change-over from acid to basic magmas after the emplacement of the acid plutonic rocks. Partly from the field evidence, partly from what seemed to follow logically from a consideration of the succession of magmas, the general sequence of the various intrusive assemblages was interpreted by Harker, as set out below:

I. Plutonic Phase:
    (i) Ultrabasic rocks, Sgùrr Dubh, Cuillin Hills.
    (ii) Gabbro, Cuillin Hills and Broadford ⎰ with hybrid rocks on Marsco,
    (iii) Granophyre and granite, Red Hills ⎱   etc.

II. Phase of Minor Intrusions:
    (i) Composite sills and dykes.
    (ii) Regional basic sills, intruded into Mesozoic strata and Tertiary basalt lavas.
    (iii) Minor acid intrusions, Red Hills area.
    (iv) Porphyritic basalt dykes of Beinn Dearg, Red Hills.
    (v) Basic dykes and inclined sheets (cone-sheets), Cuillin Hills.
    (vi) Minor ultrabasic intrusions, mainly Cuillin Hills.
    (vii) Trachyte and trachyandesite dykes of Sleat. and trachyte dykes, Drynoch.
    (viii) Pitchstone, tholeiite and augite-andesite dykes, chiefly Red Hills.
    (ix) Basic north-west dykes, of various ages.

The order in which the minor intrusions are detailed above is supported by the actual observation of intersections of one kind of intrusion by another, chiefly in the Cuillin area.

The complex of Central Skye would appear to include three intrusion-centres. These are indicated by the form and distribution of the plutonic masses within the Cuillin Hills and the western and the eastern Red Hills (Fig. 44). A Cuillin centre is also well marked by the arrangement of the minor intrusions within this area (Fig. 45).

(a) **Cuillin Hills.** The gabbro of which the Cuillin Hills are mainly composed usually contains olivine, and is especially rich in labradorite feldspar. A general laccolithic form for the gabbro mass was inferred by Harker from its relations to adjacent basalt lavas. These surround the gabbro on all sides except to the east, where there is a great intrusive lobe of the Red Hills granophyre. The gabbro overlies the basalt lavas with its base inclined at a low angle towards the interior. According to Harker, it consists of a large number of individual intrusive sheets. Around the outer part of the complex lenticular masses of older rocks, chiefly basalt lavas, mark the intrusive edges of certain of the gabbro sheets, and are gently inclined inwards (Fig. 46). But an inward inclination at higher angles (30 to 50 degrees or more) is disclosed by a conspicuous and regular banding in the arcuate ultrabasic mass of Sgùrr Dubh, and in the

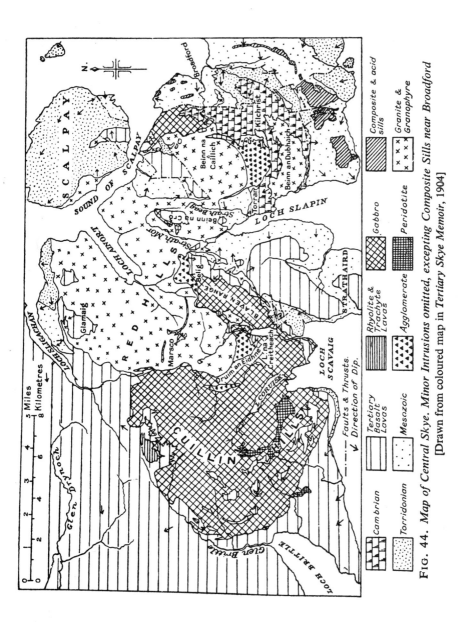

FIG. 44. *Map of Central Skye. Minor Intrusions omitted, excepting Composite Sills near Broadford*

[Drawn from coloured map in *Tertiary Skye Memoir*, 1904]

G

gabbro itself east of Sgùrr Dubh (Fig. 45). The ultrabasic rocks of Sgurr Dubh, arranged in order of an increasing amount of olivine, are: (1) picrite (with augite in addition to olivine) and allivalite (olivine-anorthite rock), (2) peridotite, (3) dunite. The gabbro banding is considered to be, in general, parallel to the surfaces of individual gabbro-sheets. The interior of the complex therefore would appear to differ in shape from that of a typical flat-based laccolith. Banding in the gabbro near Druim Hain (Druim an Eidhne) has been ascribed to gravity stratification during crystallization (1947c). From evidence seen on Druim an Eidhne, E. B. Bailey has inferred that the Cuillin gabbro is not a laccolith but a confluent cone-sheet complex (1945).

High-grade thermal metamorphism due to gabbroic and peridotitic rocks has converted adjacent lavas, and xenolithic lava masses, into basic granular hornfelses, often with relict amygdales (1904, 1931). Controversy has arisen over the origin of certain rocks which are associated with patches of lava

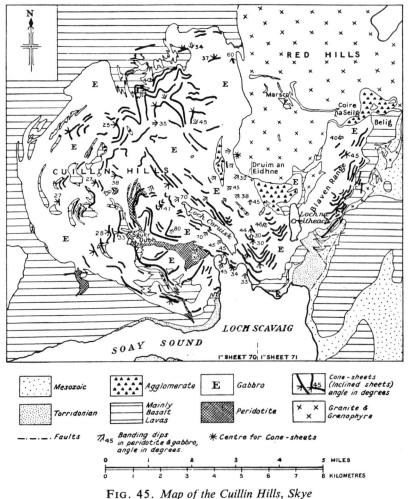

FIG. 45. *Map of the Cuillin Hills, Skye*

[Drawn from 1-inch Sheet 70 Geol. Surv. Scotland]

enveloped by gabbro at Coire Lagan and which contain alleged amygdales (1952, 1952*a*).

According to Harker, minor intrusions restricted to the Cuillin Hills, in order of their probable age, consist of: (1) a tangential set of basic dykes; (2) a radial set of basic dykes; (3) basic inclined sheets (cone-sheets); (4) a radial set of ultrabasic dykes. These intrusions are arranged with reference to approximately the same central point as that indicated by the sheets of the plutonic complex. The cone-sheets are especially remarkable (Plate VIIIB) and form one of the most complete suites known to science. The belt, however, is not continued into the granophyre area to the east. Unlike the cone-sheets of Mull and Ardnamurchan, the Cuillin sheets tend to occur singly. They are often inclined at about 45 degrees, but as a general rule their inclination becomes steeper towards the interior of the gabbro and more gentle towards its periphery. The prevalent rock-type is olivine-free dolerite.

The great majority of the ultrabasic dykes have a roughly west-east trend (1948*b*). The fabric of a dunite dyke with aligned olivines has been investigated (1938); this dyke, in Coire Lagan, is believed to be one which influenced N. L. Bowen in postulating gravitative concentration of olivine crystals to account for the origin of bodies of peridotite in the Hebrides and elsewhere (1928).

(*b*) **Western Red Hills.** The acid mass forming the Red Hills consists of a number of injections, direct evidence of which is supplied by the fact that the normal granophyre is found locally to grade into a fine-grained spherulitic rock, a chilled edge in contact with a presumably earlier granophyre. Similar spherulitic rocks are developed where the granophyre is in contact with the Cuillin gabbro. Variations in composition indicate the occurrence of different intrusions. The prevalent type is hornblende-granophyre or hornblende-granite, but there are also types characterized by having riebeckite or biotite as their distinctive ferromagnesian mineral. Four distinctive granites or granophyres have now been recognized (1946, 1948*b*).

The granophyre mass forming the western Red Hills has been described as constituting a complex laccolith. A roof is seen in places, but no floor is exposed. Dyke-like masses of gabbro extending across Marsco (Plate VIII A) and earlier than two granophyre intrusions bounding them have been interpreted in two ways. Harker (1904) considered them collectively to represent one of the feeders

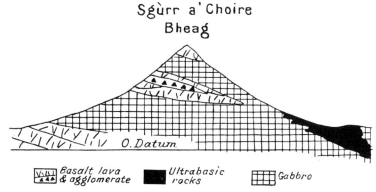

Sgùrr a' Choire
Bheag

Basalt lava & agglomerate   Ultrabasic rocks   Gabbro

FIG. 46. *Section across Southern Portion of the Cuillin Hills, Skye*
[Redrawn from part of Fig. 4, ' The Geology of West-Central Skye, with Soay ' (*Mem. Geol. Surv.*), 1904]

for the gabbro-laccolith of the Cuillin Hills. On the other hand, it has been pointed out that the Marsco gabbro resembles the screens composed of older rocks which in Mull and elsewhere separate adjacent ring-dykes (1927).

The western Red Hills are not traversed by many minor intrusions. A group of basic dykes is noteworthy, which contain porphyritic olivine and labradorite feldspar (Beinn Dearg type).

(c) **Eastern Red Hills.** The granophyres and granites of this district are concentrated around the conspicuous summit of Beinn na Caillich. The boss-like form of this granophyre mass is apparent in its steep and curved margin to the south and west; on the north the regularity of this outcrop is broken by a faulted mass of older rocks, mainly basalt lavas. The granophyre is later than the large Kilchrist volcanic vent and the extensive Broadford gabbro, to the south and north-east respectively. The vent is grouped in time with the early explosive phase of Skye (p. 51) and the gabbro with the Cuillin gabbro.

The Beinn an Dubhaich granite (1949, 1951, 1954b) is intruded into the centre of a curving anticline of Cambrian limestone and dolomite and its intrusive contacts are most intricate (Fig. 47). The granite has marmorized adjacent

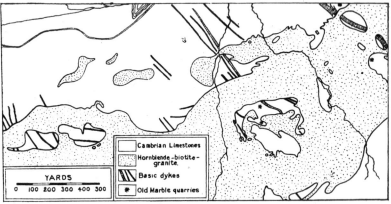

FIG. 47. *Map of Part of Beinn an Dubhaich Granite, Skye*
[Rep. from the *Tertiary Skye Memoir*, 1904, Fig. 29]

calcareous rocks, with the formation of brucite- and forsterite-marbles (1904, 1949b) and has produced remarkable boron/fluorine contact-metasomatic effects (1948, 1948a, 1949a, 1951). Skarn minerals include iron-wollastonite, chondrodite, clinohumite, humite, cuspidine, fluoborite, szaibelyite, datolite, ludwigite, harkerite and monticellite. Masses of magnetite ore are developed locally at the contact (p. 117).

The Broadford gabbro is in general free from olivine and contains much less alumina, lime and soda than the Cuillin gabbro (1953b). Like the Beinn an Dubhaich granite it has very intricate contacts with marmorized Cambrian limestone and dolomite. The three-dimensional form of the gabbro, and its petrogenesis, have been subjects of speculation (1904, 1953b).

Of the minor intrusions of the Red Hills area listed on p. 88, the composite sills attain their greatest development in the eastern district, and are classic examples of this remarkable type of intrusion. They consist usually of narrow basic margins, composed of olivine-free basalt with porphyritic feldspars, and of more massive central portions of granophyre. They illustrate the features already detailed as characteristic of composite intrusions (p. 59). Additional points of interest are: the local absence of one, or both, of the basic margins, due to their destruction by the intruding acid magma; and the frequent occurrence of xenocrysts (crystals foreign to the rock in which they are found) in the basic margins.The xenocrysts correspond to the phenocrysts (porphyritic crystals) of the acid interior portions of the intrusions. They are usually of quartz, alkali-feldspar and oligoclase feldspar; in one instance, the sill of Rudh' an Eireannaich (1959), quartz is absent in the acid interior and in the basic margins. Two classes of xenocrysts have been recognized by Harker: (1) those included in the basic magma before intrusion (antecedent), and (2) those introduced after the emplacement of the basic magma (consequent).

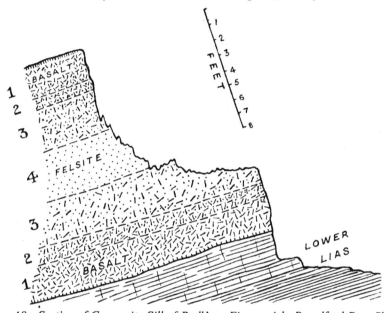

FIG. 48. *Section of Composite Sill of Rudh' an Eireannaich, Broadford Bay, Skye*

Zone 1: Basalt, with chilled edge, becoming slightly modified internally by addition of acid magma.
Zone 2: Mixed rock, grading rapidly inwards to a composition equivalent to a mixture of half basalt, half felsite, magma.
Zone 3: Mixed rock, becoming gradually more acid internally.
Zone 4: Felsite.
NOTE—The gradation from basalt to felsite is *continuous*.
[Re-drawn, with additions, from Fig. 49, *Tertiary Skye Memoir*, 1904]

(*d*) **Hybridization.** There are many examples in Central Skye of the intermingling of, and reaction between, acid and basic materials, one or both of which were in the liquid state. On Marsco (1948*b*) and elsewhere a hybrid rock, termed (for convenience of description) marscoite, was claimed by Harker as an instance of the acidification of a basic magma by the inclusion of granitic material, the resulting hybrid magma being subsequently intruded into its present position. The hybrid rock concerned occurs as lenticles in the granophyres and as narrow strips separating the gabbro masses on Marsco from the adjoining granophyres. It is characterized by containing large phenocrysts of labradorite set in a somewhat basic groundmass, in which quartz is also usually present. There has been controversy concerning the relationship between the marscoites and granitic rocks of Marsco (1947, 1947*a*, 1947*b*).

Acidification of basic magma is again met with in many basic dykes and in the basic margins of the composite sheets, which contain xenocrysts derived from a granitic or granophyric source. By the partial or complete absorption of the foreign material before the crystallization-temperature was reached, local modifications of the basic magma have been produced. These lead to the development of a finer texture and to the occurrence of a more acid plagioclase feldspar than that found in the normal rock.

An instance of the intermixing of acid and basic magmas is supplied by the composite sill of Rudh' an Eireannaich, on the north side of Broadford Bay. There is a continuous variation in composition from margins of olivine-free dolerite to a central band of felsite (Fig. 48). The two extreme types have apparently been intermixed when in the liquid state (1904, 1959).

The modification of acid magma by the incorporation of basic materials is encountered, for example, on Marsco where granophyre is in contact with the gabbro or with the hybrid marscoite. Xenoliths of the basic rock enclosed in the granophyre have been acidified, with the alteration of augite to hornblende and the introduction of alkali-feldspar and quartz. The granophyre is richer in hornblende and in oligoclase feldspar near the contact than elsewhere. Chemical analysis of the basified granophyre shows that it does not correspond simply to a mixture of the normal gabbro and granophyre, but that there has been a selective effect, due to the diffusion of different constituents from xenoliths to magma, and vice versa, at different rates.

(e) **Basic Sills.** Massive olivine-dolerite and crinanite sills younger than local Mesozoic strata occur on Raasay (1935), on the east and north coasts of Trotternish in Skye (1932, 1935–40, 1948b) and on the Shiant Isles in the North Minch (1930); they also form a number of small islets and skerries between Trotternish and the Shiants (1931a). The occurrence of picrite at or near the bases of sills is attributed by F. Walker and C. F. Davidson to gravitative concentration of crystals of olivine. In the Eilean Mhuire sill of the Shiants Walker inferred that felsic schlieren were formed by the auto-intrusion of residual magma. H. I. Drever and R. Johnston have corrected some of Walker's field observations and have questioned some of his inferences; they ascribe the schlieren of Eilean Mhuire to rhythmic crystal layering (1953, 1953a, 1957). Repeated gravitative concentration of olivine, accompanied by upward migration of alkalis, etc., has been suggested to account for remarkable rhythmic banding in the feldspathic peridotite sill of Gars-bheinn, Skye (1959a).

REFERENCES (see also p. 110)

1896. A. HARKER. On certain Granophyres, modified by the incorporation of Gabbro-fragments, in Strath (Skye). *Quart. Journ. Geol. Soc.*, vol. lii, pp. 320–328.

1904. A. HARKER. The Tertiary Igneous Rocks of Skye. *Mem. Geol. Surv.*

1904a. C. T. CLOUGH and A. HARKER. The Geology of West-Central Skye. *Mem. Geol. Surv.*

1910. C. T. CLOUGH and others. The Geology of Glenelg, Lochalsh and South-east Part of Skye. *Mem. Geol. Surv.*

1927. H. H. THOMAS. The Tertiary Plutonic Centres of Great Britain. *Rep. Brit. Assoc.* (Leeds), pp. 43–57. (Red Hills, p. 48).

1928. N. L. BOWEN. *The Evolution of the Igneous Rocks.* Princeton.

1930. F. WALKER. The Geology of the Shiant Isles (Hebrides). *Quart. Journ. Geol. Soc.*, vol. lxxxvi, pp. 355–396.

1931. A. G. MacGregor. Scottish Pyroxene-granulite Hornfelses and Odenwald Beerbachites *Geol. Mag.*, vol. lxviii, pp. 506–521.
1931a. F. Walker. The Dolerite Isles of the North Minch. *Trans. Roy. Soc. Edin.*, vol. lvi, pt. iii, pp. 753–766.
1932. F. Walker. Differentiation in the Sills of Northern Trotternish (Skye). *Trans. Roy. Soc. Edin.*, vol. lvii, pt. i, pp. 241–257.
1934. T. C. Day. An Intrusive Junction between Jurassic Sandstones and Tertiary Granite, South-east of Dunan, Isle of Skye. *Trans. Edin. Geol. Soc.*, vol. xiii, pt. i, pp. 57–60.
1935. C. F. Davidson. The Tertiary Geology of Raasay, Inner Hebrides. *Trans. Roy. Soc. Edin.*, vol. lviii, pt. ii, pp. 375–407. (Basic and acid sills, pp. 378, 388.)
1935–40. G. V. Wilson and others. *In* Summaries of Progress of the Geological Survey (*Mems. Geol. Surv.*): for 1934, Pt. I, pp. 70–71; for 1935, Pt. I, pp. 81–84; for 1936, Pt. I, pp. 77–79; for 1937, pp. 73–74; for 1938, pp. 74–76. (Basic sills.)
1938. F. C. Phillips. Mineral Orientation in some Olivine-rich Rocks from Rhum and Skye. *Geol. Mag.*, vol. lxxv, pp. 130–135.
1945. E. B. Bailey. Tertiary Igneous Tectonics of Rhum (Inner Hebrides). *Quart. Journ. Geol. Soc.*, vol. c, for 1944, pp. 165–188. (Cuillin gabbro, Skye, p. 169.)
1946. J. E. Richey, F. H. Stewart and L. R. Wager. Age relations of certain Granites and Marscoite in Skye. *Geol. Mag.*, vol. lxxxiii, p. 293.
1947. E. B. Bailey. Chilled and ' Baked ' Edges as Criteria of Relative Age. *Geol. Mag.*, vol. lxxxiv, pp. 126–128.
1947a. D. B. MacIntyre and D. L. Reynolds. Chilled and ' Baked ' Edges as Criteria of Relative Age. *Geol. Mag.*, vol. lxxxiv, pp. 61–64.
1947b. J. E. Richey, F. H. Stewart and L. R. Wager. Age Relations of certain Granites in Skye. *Geol. Mag.*, vol. lxxxiv, p. 128.
1947c. F. H. Stewart and L. R. Wager. Gravity Stratification in the Cuillin Gabbro of Skye. *Geol. Mag.*, vol. lxxxiv, p. 374.
1948. C. E. Tilley. Dolomite Contact Skarns of the Broadford Area, Skye: A Preliminary Note. *Geol. Mag.*, vol. lxxxv, pp. 213–216.
1948a. C. E. Tilley. On Iron-Wollastonites in Contact Skarns: An Example from Skye. *Amer. Min.*, vol. 33, pp. 736–738.
1948b. L. R. Wager, F. H. Stewart and F. W. Anderson. *In* Skye and Morar. *Internat. Geol. Congress, 18th Session, Gt. Brit. 1948. Guide to Excursion* C14, pp. 3–19.
1949. C. E. Tilley. An Alkali Facies of Granite at Granite-Dolomite Contacts in Skye. *Geol. Mag.*, vol. lxxxvi, pp. 81–93.
1949a. C. E. Tilley. Cupsidine from Dolomite Contact Skarns, Broadford, Skye. *Mineralogical Mag.*, vol. xxviii, pp. 90–95.
1949b. C. E. Tilley. Earlier Stages in the Metamorphism of Siliceous Dolomites. *Mineralogical Mag.*, vol. xxviii, pp. 272–276.
1951. C. E. Tilley. The Zoned Contact-Skarns of the Broadford Area, Skye: a Study of Boron–Fluorine Metasomatism in Dolomites. *Mineralogical Mag.*, vol. xxix, pp. 621–666.
1952. E. B. Bailey. So-called Amygdaloidal Gabbro, Skye. *Geol. Mag.*, vol. lxxxix, pp. 369–375.
1952a. D. L. Reynolds. So-called Amygdaloidal Gabbro, Skye: Comments on a Paper by E. B. Bailey. *Geol. Mag.*, vol. lxxxix, pp. 376–379.
1953. H. I. Drever. A Note on the Field Relations of the Shiant Isles Picrite. *Geol. Mag.*, vol. xc, pp. 159–160.
1953a. R. Johnston. The Olivines of the Garbh Eilean Sill, Shiant Isles. *Geol. Mag.*, vol. xc, pp. 161–171.
1953b. B. C. King. Structure and Igneous Activity in the Creag Strollamus Area of Skye. *Trans. Roy. Soc. Edin.*, vol. lxii, pt. ii, pp. 357–402.

1953c. L. R. WAGER, D. S. WEEDON and E. A. VINCENT. A Granophyre from Coire Uaigneich, Isle of Skye, containing Quartz Paramorphs after Tridymite. *Mineralogical Mag.*, vol. xxx, pp. 263–276.

1954. G. P. BLACK. The Significance of Tridymite in Igneous and Metamorphic Petrogenesis. *Mineralogical Mag.*, vol. xxx, pp. 518–524. (Skye, pp. 521–523.)

1954a. R. J. MURRAY. The Clinopyroxenes of the Garbh Eilean Sill, Shiant Isles. *Geol. Mag.*, vol. xci, pp. 17–31.

1954b. O. F. TUTTLE and M. L. KEITH. The Granite Problem: Evidence from the Quartz and Feldspar of a Tertiary Granite. *Geol. Mag.*, vol. xci, pp. 61–72.

1955. Y. M. ANWAR. A Clinopyroxene from the Granophyre of Meall Dearg, Skye. *Geol. Mag.*, vol. xcii, pp. 367–373.

1955a. G. P. BLACK. The Junction between Jurassic Sandstones and Tertiary Granophyre near Dunan, Isle of Skye: A Re-interpretation. *Trans. Edin. Geol. Soc.*, vol. xvi, pt. iii, pp. 217–222.

1957. H. I. DREVER. A note on the Occurrence of Rhythmic Layering in the Eilean Mhuire Sill, Shiant Isles. *Geol. Mag.*, vol. xciv, pp. 277–280.

1959. D. S. BUIST. The Composite Sill of Rudh' an Eireannaich, Skye. *Geol. Mag.*, vol. xcvi, pp. 247–252.

1959a. D. S. WEEDON. The Gars-bheinn Sill, Isle of Skye. *Quart. Journ., Geol. Soc.*, vol. cxvi, pp. 37–50.

5. ISLAND OF RUM

One of the most attractive of the Tertiary districts in the West of Scotland is marked by that beautiful mountain-group carved out of the plutonic rocks of Rum (Fig. 49). For many years few geologists set foot upon the island, but visits paid at long intervals by MacCulloch, Judd, Geikie and especially by Harker (1908)* brought to light its many diversities of structure and rock-type. More recently E. B. Bailey (1945) has reviewed many of the island's problems; Tomkeieff (1945a) and Wager and Brown (1951, 1956) have investigated the basic and ultrabasic intrusions, and G. P. Black (1952, 1954) has described the granitic and granophyric rocks that form a large outcrop to the west (Fig. 5). It is now believed that a ring-fault bounds the plutonic complex (with some peripheral Torridonian and Lewisian) on the south and east and that a reversed fault forms the northern boundary of the main granitic outcrop.

The sequence of intrusion closely resembles that described from Central Skye. Breccias, once regarded by Harker as due to crushing, have been identified as products of volcanic explosion and assigned to a post-basalt lava

FIG. 49. *General View of Rum, from the North-west*
[Rep. from ' The Geology of the Small Isles of Inverness-shire ' (*Mem. Geol. Surv.*), 1908, Fig. 20]

and pre-plutonic vent-phase (1945). Plutonic masses, ranging in time from ultrabasic to acid types, were succeeded by suites of minor intrusions. The latter

* Dates within brackets refer to References on p. 99.

include two centrally related groups, namely, a set of radial basic dykes and a somewhat sparsely developed set of basic cone-sheets. These are arranged with reference approximately to the same point as centre, situated towards the head of Glen Harris, in the middle of the ultrabasic and basic plutonic area (Fig. 50).

The plutonic rocks include a greater development of ultrabasic types than is met with elsewhere in Britain. They include allivalite composed essentially of olivine and anorthite, peridotite largely of olivine together with anorthite, and a variety of the latter (harrisite) with a lustrous black olivine. There are also masses of eucrite, with bytownite or anorthite felspar, and gabbro.

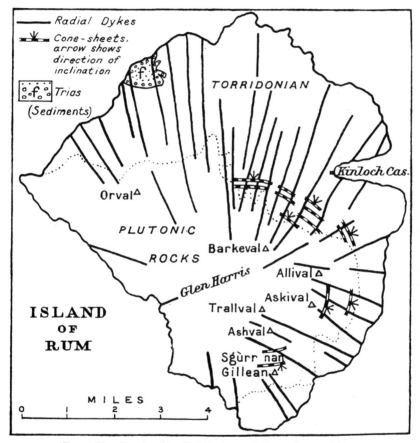

FIG. 50. *Trends of Radial Dykes and Cone-sheets of Rum*
[Based on Geological Survey maps, with addition of Trias]

The complex formed of the ultrabasic and basic masses is roughly circular. Its relations to the surrounding Torridonian grits and shales are in part steeply transgressive. The most striking structural feature, however, of the plutonic assemblage is an alternation of bands of allivalite and peridotite on the mountain slopes of Allival and Askival eastwards of the head of Glen Harris, towards which the bands are usually inclined at gentle angles (Fig. 51). According to G. M. Brown each band or sheet is composed of peridotite graduating upwards into allivalite, and the layering is due to rhythmic accumulation of a crystal

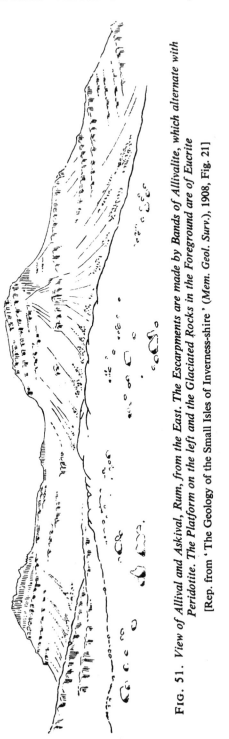

FIG. 51. *View of Allival and Askival, Rum, from the East. The Escarpments are made by Bands of Allivalite, which alternate with Peridotite. The Platform on the left and the Glaciated Rocks in the Foreground are of Eucrite* [Rep. from 'The Geology of the Small Isles of Inverness-shire' (*Mem. Geol. Surv.*), 1908, Fig. 21]

precipitate on the floor of a sub-crustal magma chamber. The layered rock body was later invaded by transgressive intrusions of gabbro and eucrite, mainly in the form of sheets.

The relations of the ultrabasic group to the country rocks are almost everywhere unknown, owing to an intervening intrusion of gabbro and eucrite (Fig. 5). To the north, however, where the main peridotite comes into contact with the Torridonian grits, its margins are steeply transgressive, as also are those of adjoining isolated masses of this rock. The eucrite and gabbro in turn are later than the ultrabasic rocks. Often contacts are extremely intricate, and the younger rock has penetrated the older in a network of ramifying veins forming a zone of *intrusion-breccia*, as it is termed. These zones range up to 100 yards in width, and are met with along the intrusive contacts of ultrabasic, basic and acid masses. Banding is prevalent in the harrisite to the west and in the adjoining large area of peridotite. In general, the bands dip towards the point near the head of Glen Harris towards which the stratiform rocks to the east are also inclined. The peripheral mass of eucrite and gabbro is in part steeply transgressive in its relations to the Torridonian, resembling a ring-dyke, but in part forms sheets traversing the stratiform ultrabasic group. West of the centre of the complex a large mass of eucrite and gabbro presents steep contacts against banded peridotite.

Where granophyre adjoins eucrite, hornblende-gneisses with highly inclined foliation are often met with. The gneisses have been interpreted in two ways, as a product of the injection of eucrite by acid magma, and as Lewisian Gneiss (p. 7). The latter conclusion has recently been confirmed and the view that the gneiss has been brought up along steeply inclined fractures has been advanced (1944, 1945).

The largest acid mass is situated in the west (Fig. 5). According to G. P. Black, it consists of a core of hornblende-microgranite and a broad margin of hornblende-granophyre. The contact of the acid rocks with adjacent basic and ultrabasic intrusions appears to be inclined steeply eastwards. On the north the boundary (against Torridonian) is almost everywhere (1954), or everywhere (1957), a reversed fault inclined to the south. Black's claim that the acid rocks represent Torridonian sandstone transformed *in situ* into granophyre (1954) has not been supported by subsequent investigators (1957).

A mass of quartz-felsite forms Sgùrr nan Gillean on the southern side of the ultrabasic complex. Similar smaller masses occur to the east and north. The rock is marked by flow structure inconstant in direction and often highly inclined. Bailey has recently grouped these rocks with the vents. The dykes of the radial set are composed of dolerite, with or without olivine, and sometimes containing porphyritic feldspars.

Cone-sheets of quartz-dolerite and basalt are sparsely distributed around the eastern half of the ultrabasic complex (Fig. 50). Individual sheets are only a few feet in width, and their inclination varies in different localities from 20 to 55 degrees. Several instances of sheets intersecting basic dykes have been observed.

REFERENCES (see also p. 110)

1908. A. HARKER. The Geology of the Small Isles of Inverness-shire. *Mem. Geol. Surv.*

1938. F. C. PHILLIPS. Mineral Orientation in some Olivine-rich Rocks from Rum and Skye. *Geol. Mag.*, vol. lxxv, pp. 130–135.

1944. C. E. TILLEY. A Note on the Gneisses of Rhum. *Geol. Mag.*, vol. lxxxi, pp. 129–131.

1945. E. B. BAILEY. Tertiary Igneous Tectonics of Rhum (Inner Hebrides). *Quart. Journ. Geol. Soc.*, vol. c for 1944, pp. 165–188.

1945a. S. I. TOMKEIEFF. On the Petrology of the Ultrabasic and Basic Rocks of the Isle of Rum. *Mineralogical Mag.*, vol. xxvii, pp. 127–136.

1951. L. R. WAGER and G. M. BROWN. A note on Rhythmic Layering in the Ultrabasic Rocks of Rhum. *Geol. Mag.*, vol. lxxxviii, pp. 166–168.

1952. G. P. BLACK. The Age Relationship of the Granophyre and Basalt of Orval, Isle of Rhum. *Geol. Mag.*, vol. lxxxix, pp. 106–112.

1954. G. P. BLACK. The Acid Rocks of Western Rhum. *Geol. Mag.*, vol. xci, pp. 257–272.

1956. G. M. BROWN. The Layered Ultrabasic Rocks of Rhum, Inner Hebrides. *Phil. Trans. Roy. Soc., Lond.*, Series B, vol. 240, pp. 1–53.

1956a. E. B. BAILEY. Hebridean Notes: Rhum and Skye. *Liverp. & Manch. Geol. Journ.*, vol. 1, pt. v, pp. 420–426.

1957. C. J. HUGHES, W. J. WADSWORTH and C. H. EMELEUS. The Contact between Tertiary Granophyre and Torridonian Arkose on Minishal, Isle of Rhum. *Geol. Mag.*, vol. xciv, pp. 337–338.

6. ISLANDS OF ST. KILDA* AND ROCKALL

(*a*) **St. Kilda.** St. Kilda is the largest of a remote group of islands, all of which are composed of Tertiary igneous rocks. The group is situated some fifty miles west of the Outer Hebrides and about a hundred miles from the mainland of Scotland. It is therefore far distant from the chain of Tertiary plutonic districts which form the main subjects for this memoir. No doubt the islands represent only a small portion of what was once an extensive intrusive complex, but the information they afford is too meagre for any conclusion to be reached as to the structure of the whole. A similarity between its rock-types and those of the island-districts of the Inner Hebrides has been known since the classic explorations of MacCulloch, to whom and to Sir Archibald Geikie our knowledge of St. Kilda was for many years mainly due. A geological survey was made in 1927 and 1928 by A. M. Cockburn (1935)†, who also assisted John Mathieson in his construction of a topographical map later issued by the Ordnance Survey. We are indebted to Cockburn for the geological map (Fig. 52).

The islands of the St. Kilda group are composed of eucrite, gabbros and dolerites invaded by three different granophyres. In addition, there is a numerous assemblage of sheets and a smaller number of dykes. The complete absence of sedimentary and volcanic rocks renders it impossible to interpret the form taken by the oldest and most widely distributed plutonic intrusion (the eucrite), except in so far as internal structures may bear a relation to the boundaries of the mass concerned.

Geikie came to the conclusion that the St. Kilda eucrite was built of a number of sills or sheets. The truncated ends of these sheets were regarded by him as constituting the great cliff-scarps along the western coasts of St. Kilda, the the Dùn and Soay, with a dominant north-easterly dip varying in amount from 15 to 60 degrees. In Boreray an opposite direction of dip, i.e. to south-west, is suggested in his writings. On the other hand, Cockburn scaled the cliffs at numerous points and was not able to confirm Geikie's conclusions in this

---

* The account of St. Kilda is quoted, with little change, from ' Tertiary Ring Structures in Britain ', *Trans. Geol. Soc., Glasgow*, vol. xix, part i, 1932, pp. 83–86.

† Dates within brackets refer to References on p. 103.

particular. He states that only one type of rock is present, namely, a rather fine-textured eucrite, but that varietal forms of eucrite and inextensive sheets of granulitic gabbro and gabbro-pegmatite are crossed in such traverses. While Geikie's conception of the nature of the mass must be discarded, there remains the internal evidence observed by Cockburn. There are other structural lines on St. Kilda, all of which conform to the same general alignment, i.e. north-west—south-east.

In the eucrite itself, the sparse granulite strips and the bands of pegmatite extend north-west and dip at angles of some 60 degrees north-eastwards. In parallelism with these a faint banding is sometimes to be observed in the eucrite. Some of the granulites recall similar elongate inclusions in other Tertiary gabbros, in Ardnamurchan (hypersthene-gabbro) and in Mull (gabbro of Ben Buie). Those in Ardnamurchan are also parallel to banding. Perhaps the St. Kilda occurrences are likewise xenolithic in origin. They supply an indication

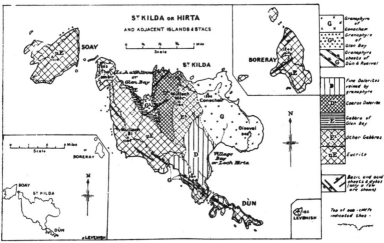

FIG. 52. *Map of St. Kilda Group of Islands*
(Geology by A. M. Cockburn)
[Rep., with alterations, from ' Tertiary Ring Structures in Britain ', *Trans. Geol. Soc., Glasgow*, vol. xix, part i, 1932, Fig. 11]

of what may have been the shape of the eucrite itself, if we may assume that the flow of the magma during intrusion was parallel to the walls of the intrusion-cavity. Regular-running bands of pegmatite like those of St. Kilda are prevalent in the Great Eucrite of Ardnamurchan, in which the bands are parallel to adjoining margins of this massive ring-dyke, and are in general vertical or else very steeply inclined. In the Ardnamurchan memoir they have been inter-preted as the infillings of contraction-cracks developed in the cooling mass parallel to its margins, derived from still-liquid portions in which fluxes had become concentrated. A similar explanation applied to the St. Kilda occur-rences supports the other evidence just cited of a somewhat steep inclination of the eucrite to the north-east. On Boreray, which lies four miles to the north-east of St. Kilda, Cockburn was not able to find any internal structures to suggest what the external form of the eucrite may there have been.

A north-westerly orientation of the post-eucrite intrusions of St. Kilda is shown by the following junctions. The dolerite mapped on the north side of the

Dun and farther north-westward in St. Kilda includes four different types of rock, alike in that all are much veined by granophyre (1953a), which unfortunately obscures any evidence there may be of their mutual relationships. But Cockburn ascertained that the junction of the mass, taken as a unit, with the eucrite extends north-westwards from the Dùn to beyond Ruaival, and dips steeply to the south-west. Farther north the dolerite appears to be plunging northwards beneath the eucrite.

A steep inclination to the south-west is also encountered in the case of the three granophyres which Cockburn distinguished. To the north the Glen Bay mass (G^1 of Fig. 52) is thus inclined in contact with olivine-poor gabbro into which it is intruded, and which forms a narrow outcrop around it. Further, a narrow elongate intrusion of the same rock just west of the main mass is similarly inclined. The olivine-poor gabbro is shattered in proximity to the contact of the granophyre, and there is an alignment of the shattered material north-westwards, with dip to the south-west at a high angle, parallel, in fact, to the intrusive contact of the granophyre. This shattering is considered to have preceded the intrusion of the granophyre itself, though the latter is also shattered to some extent. Along the cliffs on the south-west coast of St. Kilda and extending into the Dùn two broad sheets of granophyre have been traced. They are steeply inclined, like the Glen Bay mass, to the south-west. Their walls likewise are highly shattered, and there is also some recrystallization of the finely broken material.

Lastly, the well-known granophyre of Conachair and Oiseval, forming the eastern part of St. Kilda, is seen to be intrusive against the basic masses to the west, with a north-westerly extending margin which is mainly inclined at a high angle to the south-west. The junction is magnificently exposed in the great sea-cliff to the north of Conachair. For a space it becomes almost horizontal, but its essentially steep nature is a matter of observation.

In conclusion, it may be said that the various islands of the St. Kilda group probably lie near to the periphery of a plutonic complex, the central portion of which is no longer observable. The centre of the complex may possibly lie midway between St. Kilda and Boreray. The diameter of the complex, as measured north-eastwards from the south-west coast of St. Kilda to the farther shore of Boreray, may have been six miles. In regard to the disposition of the St. Kilda intrusive masses, the eucrite bears a resemblance to that of Ben Buie in Mull, if the internal evidence cited can be regarded as proof of an inclination towards the centre of the complex. The remaining available data concerning structure clearly indicate an inclination of intrusive margins outwards from the supposed centre. This, we have reason to believe, is the prevalent inclination of ring-dykes. That such is the form of the St. Kilda plutonic complex, however, cannot be more than suggested owing to the relict nature of the St. Kilda group.

Brief reference may be made to the minor intrusions. Of these Cockburn recognized two main age-groups on St. Kilda. The older group consists mainly of sheets which cut the Glen Bay granophyre in addition to the eucrite and dolerite, but which are absent from the later granophyre of Conachair. Upon these observations the age-relation of the two granophyres is based. Vertical or highly inclined dykes as well as more gently inclined sheets are presented, and in composition include both basic and acid types. The intrusions trend north-westwards along the western side of St. Kilda, with north-east dip, and north-eastwards with a south-east dip in the north-central portion of the island. The amount of dip of the sheets varies from 30 to 60 degrees. The later group includes dolerite dykes as well as sheets, striking mainly north-west but also in places north-east.

(*b*) **Rockall.** Rockall, an isolated conical islet 70 ft. in height, lies 190 miles westwards of St. Kilda. Its granitic nature has been known since 1814 and its alkaline character and richness in cerium and zirconium since 1914. Specimens collected during the visit of H.M.S. *Vidal* in 1955 have provided new mineralogical data (1960). The island is formed of a coarse-grained greyish aegirine-granite, with some acmite and riebeckite. The granite has numerous small miarolitic -cavities in which secondary or late-stage minerals occur; these include cristobalite, elpidite, cerium-bearing zirconosilicates, and possibly yttrocerite. A dark variety of the granite, called rockallite by J. W. Judd, occurs only as veins, segregations or cognate inclusions.

REFERENCES

1924. G. W. TYRRELL. The Geology and Petrography of Rockall. *Geol. Mag.*, vol. lxi, pp. 19–25.
1935. A. M. COCKBURN. The Geology of St. Kilda. *Trans. Roy. Soc. Edin.*, vol. lviii, pt. ii, pp. 511–547.
1953. D. L. REYNOLDS. Comments on an Article entitled ' Basic Magma chilled against Acid Magma '. *Nature*, vol. 172, pp. 69–70. (St. Kilda).
1953a. L. R. WAGER and E. B. BAILEY. Basic Magma chilled against Acid Magma. *Nature*, vol. 172, pp. 68–69. (St. Kilda).
1960. P. A. SABINE. The Geology of Rockall, North Atlantic. *Bull. Geol. Surv. Gt. Brit.* No. 16, pp. 156–178.

7. ISLAND OF ARRAN

Arran, bounded to the east by the Firth of Clyde, lies somewhat remote from the other plutonic districts to the north, and is within easy reach of the thickly populated areas of the Midland Valley of Scotland. Its varied scenery and interesting geology have attracted many investigators. The detailed mapping of the island was carried out by W. Gunn (1903)* towards the end of last century, and has formed a basis for more recent advances made by G. W. Tyrrell (1928) and others (1926, 1942, 1955). In addition to abundant dykes, there are three main intrusive assemblages of Tertiary age, as follows (Fig. 8):

(*a*) Sills of Southern Arran.
(*b*) Northern Granite.
(*c*) Central Ring Complex.

There is evidence that the Northern Granite is earlier than the Central Ring Complex. The sills have an extensive time-range. Some are considered to be the earliest intrusions in the island. Others are believed to be contemporaneous with or later than the latest intrusions of the Central Ring Complex.

(*a*) **Sills of South Arran and South Bute.** The Arran sills are intruded into Permian and Triassic strata, chiefly sandstone. They have been divided into three age-groups by Tyrrell (Fig. 53):

1. Olivine-analcite-dolerite (crinanite) sills.
2. Quartz-dolerite, craignurite and related felsite sills.
3. Quartz-porphyry, pitchstone (chiefly acid varieties) and related felsite sills.

* Dates within brackets refer to References on p. 110.

In addition, there is a large mass of augite-diorite surrounding an outcrop of microgranite on Tighvein, which may be sill-like in form.

The *crinanite sills* include four massive intrusions. Three of these form a broken circle around Lamlash, towards which they are all inclined; the fourth lies farther south. They are in part transgressive to the country rocks. For example, the Kingcross sill is inclined northwards towards Lamlash, and cuts across the bedding of the southwardly dipping Permian sandstones. All four sills finger out towards the west, and their magmatic source therefore is concluded to have lain to the east. They are uniform in composition, being similar to basalt of the Hebridean plateau type, and are considered by Tyrrell to belong to the plateau lava period. Margins are well chilled; coarse-textured (pegmatitic) varieties occur as bands, veins and patches in the interior; and white fine-grained (aplitic) veins are frequent in the Clauchlands sill.

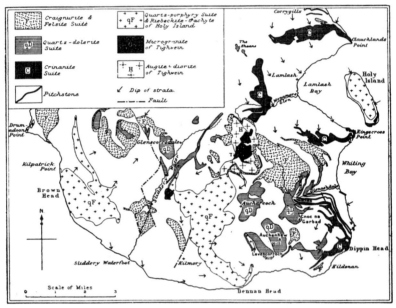

FIG. 53. *Map of South Arran, showing Tertiary Sills*
[Drawn from 1-inch Sheet 21, Geol. Surv. Scotland, with additions by G. W. Tyrrell]

The Kingcross crinanite is intruded by thin veins of quartz-dolerite, presumably derived from the same source as adjoining sills of this rock-type. For this reason the quartz-dolerite suite is considered to be of later date.

The *quartz-dolerite sills* are the most important members of an assemblage that includes also more acid rocks allied to craignurite and felsite (1928, 1958). There are several examples of composite intrusion, with margins of quartz-dolerite and more massive centres of craignurite or felsite; in some cases (Glenashdale sill) thin margins are felsitic and the central portions quartz-doleritic. An interesting sill, forming the Sheans, consists of quartz-dolerite which is traversed by a tangle of acid veins (net-veining) forming intrusion-breccias.

The sills are for the most part regular-running sheets, seldom transgressing the bedding of the country rocks. They give rise to a topography marked by

A. VIEW OF MARSCO, RED HILLS, SKYE, SHOWING TWO GRANOPHYRE INTRUSIONS
SEPARATED BY VERTICAL WALL OF GABBRO-HYBRID (FORMING GULLY)

B. VIEW OF COIRE NA CREICHE, CUILLIN HILLS, SKYE, SHOWING CONE-SHEETS
CUTTING GABBRO

A. SILL OF COLUMNAR QUARTZ-PORPHRY, WITH BASALT ALONG LOWER
CONTACT; TRIASSIC SANDSTONES BELOW. DRUMADOON, ARRAN

B. BASALTIC DYKES OF ARRAN SWARM CUTTING TRIASSIC SANDSTONES;
SHORE BETWEEN KILDONAN AND BENNAN HEAD, SOUTH COAST OF ARRAN

even scarps and flat terraces, and frequently form the 'sills' of waterfalls. Many are only some 10 ft. or so in thickness, but many are massive intrusions. For example, the multiple quartz-dolerite sill of Cnoc na Garbad is 250 ft. thick (1928, 1958). In several instances the sills become thinner when traced eastwards. Thus, in contrast with the crinanite sills, the quartz-dolerite sills may have been derived from western sources.

The *quartz-porphyry and pitchstone sills* are widely distributed throughout

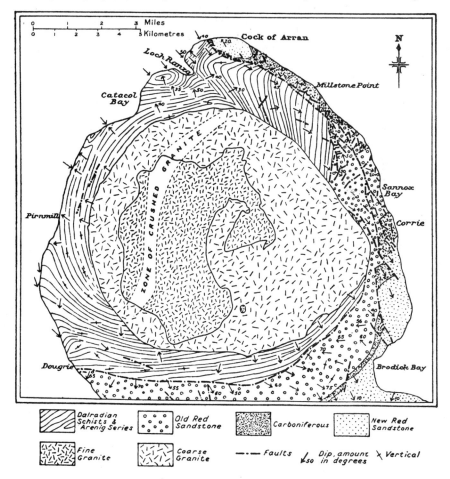

FIG. 54. *Map of Northern Granite, Arran*
[Redrawn, with modifications and omission of dykes, from Pl. III, ' The Geology of Arran '
(*Mem. Geol. Surv.*), 1928]

Arran. Some of the pitchstones cut the Northern Granite, while the quartz-porphyries can be matched with rocks intruded at a late date in the Central Ring Complex. They are probably of various ages, but all are supposed to be later than the quartz-dolerites and crinanites.

The quartz-porphyry sills are massive, but the pitchstones are relatively thin, and individual intrusions often change in form from a sill to a dyke. Both rock-types sometimes form the centres of composite intrusions with margins of a

H

basic rock, usually tholeiite. Pitchstone is frequently associated with felsite, which is concluded to be simply devitrified pitchstone. Three important sills of quartz-porphyry form respectively Bennan Head, Kilpatrick Point and Drumadoon Point (Plate IXA). Along portions of the Bennan and Drumadoon sills the intrusions are composite, with narrow basic selvedges. These margins contain, even in their chilled edges, xenocrysts similar to the phenocrysts of the acid interior portions.

In South Bute, near Garroch Head, two Tertiary sills traverse Palaeozoic strata (1940, 1952); one is crinanite and the other, which cuts across the crinanite, is a composite sheet of considerable interest. It consists of a central pyroxene-dolerite, flanked above and below by quartz-porphyry and marginal tholeiitic dolerite. D. S. Buist (1952) has described a possible mechanism of intrusion.

The sills and dykes of pitchstone are perhaps the best known rocks of Arran. They are mainly of acid composition, greenish in colour, and crowded with crystallites, often aggregated in feathery forms. Either they are non-porphyritic (Corrygills type) or they contain porphyritic feldspars (Tormore and Glen Shurig types). In the Glen Shurig type the iron-olivine, fayalite, is present. A somewhat more basic type (Glen Cloy), when devitrified, tends to develop variolitic or spherulitic structures (1914, 1928, 1928a, 1954). C. E. Tilley has recently identified biotite as the dominant mineral of the arborescent, plumose and scopulitic growths of the pitchstones (1957).

Riebeckite–trachyte forms the massive sill of Holy Island. Its base is exposed near sea-level and it has a visible thickness of over 1,000 ft. An allied, though slightly more acid, Tertiary rock is the riebeckite-microgranite of Ailsa Craig off the South Ayrshire coast. The Holy Island sill is not cut by a single dyke of the many that traverse underlying sediments. It is therefore concluded to be one of the latest intrusions of Arran. In contrast the Ailsa Craig rock is traversed by a number of basic dykes.

(b) **Northern Granite.** Northern Arran, with its high jagged summits formed of granite, is a striking scenic contrast to the lower country to the south, which is mainly eroded out of the 1,200 ft. Pliocene platform (p. 114). In the granitic tract the highest and most rugged ground, which culminates in the summit of Goatfell at 2,866 ft., is composed of an outer and older coarse-grained granite; while smoothly contoured hills to the west of the Goatfell group of peaks mark the outcrop of a central and later fine-textured granite (Fig. 54). This inner mass becomes very fine in grain at contacts with the older coarse-textured granite; it is believed to be intrusive in the outer granite (1942). Both intrusions are composed of biotite-granite. Drusy cavities lined with quartz, potash-feldspar, etc., are frequently developed throughout both masses. Other minerals found in the druses are albite, beryl, topaz, garnet and stilbite.

Both granites are traversed by close-set joints, of which there are two main kinds. There are joints parallel to the hillsides, which are possibly due to the alternate heating and cooling of the rocks during recent periods when there was a wide diurnal range in temperature. Mural jointing, resembling masonry, is encountered on isolated granite tors and scarps, and is to be ascribed either to contraction during later stages of cooling or, in part, to later crustal stresses operating on a regional scale.

The alteration of the surrounding country rocks by the heat and vapours derived from this great granite mass is as a rule not intense. The schists, however, often develop biotite, and cordierite and andalusite have also been noted.

The rocks are indurated usually for a distance of only a few hundred yards from the granite. More widespread vapour action is indicated by extensive epidote and quartz veining. The colour of the Lower Old Red Sandstone is changed from reddish-brown to greenish-grey, owing to the alteration of the iron from the ferric to the ferrous state.

On all sides of the granite great displacements have affected the surrounding rocks. These displacements consisted mainly in the pushing up of the country rocks by the granitic magma, so that their strike is now approximately parallel to the margin of the granite (1926). The uplift is apparent in the steep outward dips not only of the schists next to the granite but also of the Old Red Sandstone, Carboniferous and Permian strata near Brodick for a distance of one and three-quarter miles from the margin of the intrusion. In addition, the effects of outward pressure are apparent in a steep-sided syncline on the north-west side of the granite, and in the overturning of Lower Old Red Sandstone beds on the south-eastern side, westwards of Brodick Bay. This great dome is broken to the north-east by a fault. Along the fault the roof of the intruding granite parted from the wall, and the strata forming the wall are in consequence relatively undistorted (Fig. 55). Here only do rocks higher in the stratified sequence than the schists

SECTION ACROSS NORTH ARRAN GRANITE

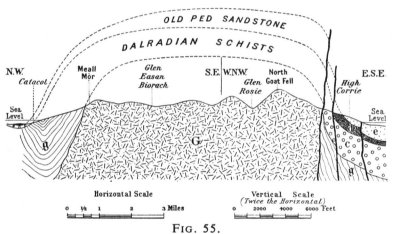

FIG. 55.

g = Dalradian Schists; c = Lower and Upper Old Red Sandstone; d = Carboniferous; e = Permian; G = Tertiary granite

[Rep., with alterations, from ' The Geology of Arran ' (*Mem. Geol. Surv.*), 1928, Fig. 21]

come directly into contact with the granite, and always with a mylonized margin. A continuation of the fault curves around the southern part of the dome, where it separates schists next to the granite from the Lower Old Red Sandstone. This portion of the fault perhaps long antedates the intrusion of the granite, by which it was deformed. It may be a direct continuation of the Highland Boundary Fault (p. 6).

(c) **Central Ring Complex.** This igneous assemblage is less than three miles in diameter, and is the smallest of the Tertiary plutonic complexes. Unlike the Northern Granite, it is composed of a great variety of rocks. It is approximately circular, but the different masses composing it are arranged in a less regular ring pattern than its external shape would suggest.

On the north-eastern side of the complex, the outermost intrusions cut across the strike of the surrounding strata, which structurally form a part of the dome around the Northern Granite. The intrusions concerned are well exposed at the head of Glen Dubh, and consist of quartz-gabbro and diorite, probably the earliest members of the Central Complex. Consequently the Central Complex is concluded to be later than the Northern Granite. A small dome is also developed around the complex itself (Fig. 8).

Explosion-breccias filling a vent occupy a large part of the Central Complex, and are mainly composed of fragments of Lower Old Red Sandstone strata. Large masses of sedimentary rocks have slipped down into the vent from a higher stratigraphical level than the Lower Old Red Sandstone, by which the Central Complex is mainly bounded. The displaced strata are proved by their fossil contents to belong to the Rhaetic, Lias and Chalk formations. Still greater vertical displacements are indicated by fragments of Tertiary basalt lavas, and by a curving screen-like mass of these lavas which separates vent-breccias from an intrusion of post-breccia felsite (Fig. 56).

The time-sequence of the various masses belonging to the Central Complex is not fully known. Probably the earliest intrusions are those composed of gabbro and diorite. They were succeeded by fine-grained granite, and a number of isolated masses of the basic plutonic rocks are enclosed in the granite. The present distribution of the basic rocks suggests that originally they extended continuously around, at any rate, the north-eastern half of the complex.

Masses of felsite and granophyre to the north-west of Ard Bheinn, in the western half of the complex, yield fragments to adjacent vent-breccias. The breccias, which form a somewhat irregular ring-shaped outcrop, are in turn earlier than the fine-grained granite. The outlines of the breccia-ring therefore mark the intrusive contact of the surrounding granite. Numerous fragments of a similar granite, however, are included in the breccias. The breccias are everywhere indurated and epidotized, presumably by the action of hot vapours, and are locally more highly contact-altered, with the formation of biotite.

Rhyolite on Ard Bheinn may represent lava-flows connected with the vent. Finally, acid magma was intruded irregularly into the vent-materials in the Ard Bheinn area, forming the later felsites shown on Fig. 56. The intrusion-centre thus appears to have shifted slightly towards the west during the formation of the Central Ring Complex.

Of the various rock-types, the gabbros and diorites are of particular interest. On the east side of the complex quartz-gabbro and olivine-gabbro are accompanied by fine-textured diorites and patchy mixture-rocks, hybrids due to the interaction of acid magma with gabbro. The formation of the hybrid magma presumably took place at some depth beneath the present surface, and was followed by its intrusion. Locally the gabbros are intersected by abundant veins of granophyre that form net-like patterns upon the rock surfaces (net-veining). The gabbro itself is altered to diorite, with the transformation of augite to hornblende.

The fine-grained granite differs from the biotite-granites of the northern massif, being richer in biotite, and containing hornblende in addition.

The explosion-breccias are unbedded tumultuous accumulations of fragments of all shapes and sizes. Since they consist mainly of broken-up country rocks, the vent would appear to have been largely choked up with such debris.

Intrusions, however, penetrating the breccias may have reached the surface and given rise to lava flows and superficial deposits of tuff and agglomerate.

The above summary is based on Tyrrell's account (1928). Recently the south-western half of the Central Complex has been re-investigated by B. C. King (1954a, 1955). He suggests that the main sequence of events may have been: (1) pre-Complex doming; (2) cauldron-subsidence, producing a great caldera; (3) general doming within the caldera, probably accompanied by peripheral

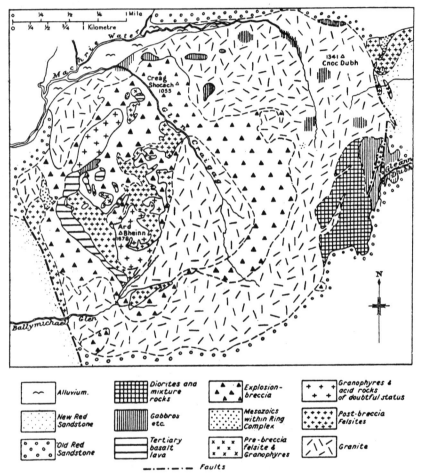

FIG. 56. *Map of Central Ring Complex, Arran*

[Redrawn, with some omissions, from Pl. IV, ' The Geology of Arran ' (*Mem. Geol. Surv.*), 1928]

subsidences along inner ring-fractures; (4) local doming associated with individ-ual explosive volcanoes that developed within the caldera and were fed by basaltic, andesitic and felsitic magma (Ard Bheinn, Binnein na h-Uaimh, Creag Dubh, Creag an Fheidh); (5) peripheral intrusion of granites guided by pre-existing arcuate structures. The limits of the supposed caldera are not fully defined and the status of much of the great arcuate outcrop of explosion-breccia (Fig. 56) appears to be left unsettled.

REFERENCES

1903. W. Gunn and others. The Geology of North Arran, South Bute and the Cumbraes. *Mem. Geol. Surv.*

1914. A. Scott. The Pitchstones of South Arran. *Trans. Geol. Soc. Glasgow*, vol. xv, pt. i, pp. 16–36.

1926. E. B. Bailey. Domes in Scotland and South Africa: Arran and Vredefort. *Geol. Mag.*, vol. lxiii, pp. 481–495.

1928. G. W. Tyrrell. The Geology of Arran. *Mem. Geol. Surv.*

1928a. P. J. Robinson. The Pitchstone Porphyry of Penrioch, Arran. *Trans. Geol. Soc. Glasgow*, vol. xviii, pt. ii, pp. 295–299.

1940. W. J. McCallien. Notes on the Geological Structure of South Bute. *Trans. Geol. Soc. Glasgow*, vol. xx, pt. i, pp. 96–102. (Tertiary sills).

1942. W. R. Flett. The Contact between the Granites of North Arran. *Trans. Geol. Soc. Glasgow*, vol. xx, pt. ii, pp. 180–203.

1948. G. W. Tyrrell. *In* Arran and South-west Scotland. *Internat. Geol. Congress, 18th Session, Gt. Brit. 1948. Guide to Excursion A*15, pp. 2–11.

1952. D. S. Buist. A contribution to the Petrochemistry and Petrogenesis of the Composite Sill of South Bute. *Trans. Edin. Geol. Soc.*, vol. xv, pp. 52–68.

1954. P. G. Harris and G. W. Brindley. Mordenite as an Alteration Product of a Pitchstone Glass. *Amer. Min.*, vol. 39, pp. 819–824. (Arran).

1954a. B. C. King. Gabbro Tuff in the Central Volcanic Complex of Arran. *Trans. Geol. Soc. Glasgow*, vol. xxi, pt. iii, pp. 440–446.

1955. B. C. King. The Ard Bheinn Area of the Central Igneous Complex of Arran. *Quart. Journ. Geol. Soc.*, vol. cx for 1954, pp. 323–354.

1957. C. E. Tilley. A Note on the Pitchstones of Arran. *Geol. Mag.*, vol. xciv, pp. 329–333.

1958. M. Spirama Rao. Composite and Multiple Intrusions of the Lamlash–Whiting Bay Region, Arran. *Geol. Mag.*, vol. xcv, pp. 265–280.

1959. M. Spirama Rao. Minor Acid Intrusions and Dykes of Lamlash–Whiting Bay Region, Arran. *Geol. Mag.*, vol. xcvi, pp. 237–246.

1960. S. I. Tomkeieff. Isle of Arran. Guide No. 32. *Geol. Assoc., London.*

1961. S. I. Tomkeieff and M. Longstaff. The Magmatic Complex at Kingscross Point, Isle of Arran. *Trans. Edin. Geol. Soc.*, vol. 18, pt. 2, pp. 194–201.

1963. J. A. Miller and W. B. Harland. Ages of Some Tertiary intrusive Rocks in Arran. *Mineralogical Mag.*, vol. 33, pp. 521–523.

ADDITIONAL REFERENCES
Skye (p. 94) and Rhum (p. 99)

1960. B. C. King. The Form of the Beinn an Dubhaich Granite, Skye. *Geol. Mag.*, vol. xcvii, pp. 326–333.

1961. E. H. T. Whitten. Modal Variation and the Form of the Beinn an Dubhaich Granite, Skye. *Geol. Mag.*, vol. xcviii, pp. 467–472.

1960. C. J. Hughes. The Southern Mountains Igneous Complex, Isle of Rhum. *Quart. J. Geol. Soc.*, vol. cxvi, pp. 111–138.

1961. W. J. Wadsworth. The Layered Ultrabasic Rocks of South-West Rhum, Inner Hebrides. *Phil. Trans. Roy. Soc. London*, Ser. B, No. 707, vol. 244, pp. 21–64.

VI. TERTIARY IGNEOUS ROCKS: NORTH-WEST DYKE-SWARMS

THE CLUSTERING OF the Tertiary north-west dykes to form swarms crossing the plutonic complexes of Skye, Mull and Arran is illustrated by Fig. 2. It will be seen that many Tertiary dykes also extend north and south as connecting links between the three Tertiary swarms (1939)*.

The dykes are especially abundant in the vicinity of the plutonic complexes, to which they are evidently related. Indeed, dykes of acid rock-types and multiple basic dykes are practically restricted to the vicinity of these areas. The basic dykes consist mainly of two contrasted suites of rocks, namely, olivine-dolerite—crinanite, and tholeiite—quartz-dolerite. F. Walker has described the type crinanite, and other rocks to which the name has been applied (1934). In describing the Tertiary dykes of Bute, H. J. W. Brown (1931) discussed the use of the terms 'crinanite' and 'tholeiite'.

As illustrations of the extraordinary abundance of dykes in the vicinity of the plutonic complexes, details from Mull (1924) and Arran (1928) are given in the following table, together with other information:

LOCALITY	BREADTH OF SWARM EXAMINED	NUMBER OF DYKES	TOTAL AGGREGATE THICKNESS OF DYKES	AVERAGE INDIVIDUAL THICKNESS OF DYKES	AMOUNT OF CRUSTAL STRETCH DUE TO DYKE INTRUSION
	mls.		ft.	ft.	
South-east coast of Mull ..	12·5	375	2,504	5·8	1 in 26·4
Arran	14·8	525	6,050	11·5	1 in 14·4

The Skye swarm crosses the Cuillin Hills and extends north-westwards to the Outer Hebrides, where a few olivine-dolerite dykes belonging to it reach South Harris and North Uist. South-eastwards, the Skye dykes end at the line of the Great Glen Fault, along Loch Linnhe.

The Mull swarm also is represented in the Outer Hebrides, where a few quartz-dolerite dykes are found in South Uist and Barra. South-eastwards it has a much greater extension (1936). The intrusions composing it continue in ever decreasing numbers across the Firth of Clyde into Ayrshire. Crossing the Southern Uplands the depleted swarm is represented in the North of England by a few solitary dykes, the direction of which gradually changes to west-north-west and finally to west-east. These extensive members of the Mull swarm are composed of quartz-dolerite and tholeiite, whereas olivine-dolerite and crinanite dykes do not continue beyond the Firth of Clyde.

The Arran swarm is of mixed origin. Olivine-dolerite and crinanite dykes extend north-westwards from this district to cross Islay and Jura, where they are much more numerous and more closely spaced than in Arran itself (1932). This assemblage, therefore, is considered to be related, not to Arran, but to a plutonic centre hidden beneath the sea somewhere to the north-west of Islay (p. 43). Tholeiite dykes trend more or less north and south across Arran and,

* Dates within brackets refer to References on p. 112.

together with others of olivine-dolerite and crinanite, are very numerous on the southern coast (Plate IXB). They are again represented farther south in Ailsa Craig and along the coast of the mainland, but do not continue far inland.

The deviation of dykes southwards from the Skye swarm to Mull, and from the Mull swarm to Arran, suggests that all three districts functioned as active igneous centres at or about the same time. When the ages of the dykes relatively to the local plutonic and hypabyssal intrusions are examined in detail, it is found that in each district the formation of the dykes extended throughout much of the period of local igneous activity, though many were intruded towards its close. In Skye many of the north-west dykes in the Cuillin Hills are cut by the cone-sheets (p. 88), and others are earlier than the Red Hills granite (e.g. Beinn an Dubhaich mass, Fig. 47). In Mull many dykes are earlier than the grano-phyres around Centre 2 (Loch Bà), but many more cut these plutonic masses and also the still later Loch Bà ring-dyke (p.72). All dykes, however, examined from Central Mull are altered by vapour action (pneumatolysis). In Arran certain crinanite or olivine-dolerite dykes can be shown to be earlier than, and altered by, the Northern Granite, and the tholeiitic dykes cut the crinanitic dykes and the Northern Granite. In Ardnamurchan dykes are numerous, though they do not appear to constitute a swarm extending beyond the limits of the area, unless the abundant dykes of the island of Muck are related to this plutonic district. In regard to their position in the local time-sequence, some are earlier than the outer cone-sheets of Centre 2 (p. 79), but others cut the latest of the plutonic intrusions.

Unusual contact phenomena at the margins of a basalt dyke cutting grano-phyric granite in Skye have been described by B. C. King (1954) and commented on by E. B. Bailey (1956); marginal mobilization of granite is invoked in one of the explanations offered.

On Maiden Island (Oban), in Ardnamurchan and on the islands of Muck and Islay, very broad, short north-westerly Tertiary dykes, or elongated bosses, of considerable interest have been described (1939a, 1947, 1947a, 1959). The Maiden Island boss consists of olivine-dolerite with local marginal picrite. The second intrusion (Ardnamurchan) is a composite quartz-dolerite/quartz-bostonite mass showing hybridization. The third (Muck) is an olivine-gabbro which is contaminated by, and produces contact-metasomatism in, Jurassic limestone; minerals developed in the limestone include wollastonite, analcite, gehlenite, monticellite, periclase, spurrite, merwinite, larnite and rankinite. The fourth (Islay) consists of analcite-olivine-leucodolerite and (localized) teschenite, which are regarded as derived by differentiation from magma similar to that of the Tertiary crinanite dykes of the district.

REFERENCES

1924. E. B. BAILEY and others. The Tertiary and Post-Tertiary Geology of Mull, Loch Aline and Oban. *Mem. Geol. Surv.*

1928. G. W. TYRRELL. The Geology of Arran. *Mem. Geol. Surv.*

1931. H. J. W. BROWN. Dykes and Associated Intrusions of the Island of Bute. *Trans. Geol. Soc. Glasgow*, vol. xviii, pt. iii, pp. 388–419. (Tertiary, pp. 397–416).

1932. W. J. McCALLIEN. The Kainozoic Igneous Rocks of Kintyre. *Geol. Mag.*, vol. lxix, pp. 49–61.

934. F. WALKER. The Term ' Crinanite '. *Geol. Mag.*, vol. lxxi, pp. 122–128.

1935. C. F. DAVIDSON. The Tertiary Geology of Raasay, Inner Hebrides. *Trans. Roy. Soc. Edin.*, vol. lviii, pt. ii, pp. 375–407. (Dykes, pp. 391–402.)

1936. A. ALLISON. The Tertiary Dykes of the Craignish Area, Argyll. *Geol. Mag.*, vol. lxxiii, pp. 73-87.

1939. J. E. RICHEY. The Dykes of Scotland. *Trans. Edin. Geol. Soc.*, vol. xiii, pt. iv, pp. 393–435. (Tertiary dykes, pp. 419–425).

1939a. F. WALKER. The Geology of Maiden Island, Oban. *Trans. Edin. Geol. Soc.*, vol. xiii, pt. iv, pp. 475–482.

1947. J. McMATH. The Composite Intrusion of Sròn Bheag, Ardnamurchan. *Geol. Mag.*, vol. lxxxiv, pp. 257–269.

1947a. C. E. TILLEY. The Gabbro-Limestone Contact Zone of Camas Mòr, Muck, Inverness-shire. *Bull. Comm. Géol. Finl.*, No. 140, pp. 97–105.

1954. B. C. KING. Contact Phenomena Associated with a Dolerite Dyke at Creag Strollamus, Skye. *Trans. Geol. Soc. Glasgow*, vol. xxi, pt. iii, pp. 436–439.

1956. E. B. BAILEY. Hebridean Notes: Rhum and Skye. *Liverp. & Manch. Geol. Journ.*, vol. 1, pt. v, pp. 420–426.

1959. F. WALKER and E. M. PATTERSON. A Differentiated Boss of Alkali Dolerite from Cnoc Rhaonastil, Islay. *Mineralogical Mag.*, vol. 32, pp. 140–152.

See also list of Geological Survey memoirs on p. 120: North Arran etc.; West-central Skye; Tertiary Igneous Rocks of Skye; Small Isles of Inverness-shire; Glenelg, Lochalsh and S.E. Skye; Colonsay, Oronsay etc.; Staffa, Iona and W. Mull; Ardnamurchan etc.

ADDITIONAL REFERENCES

1958. H. I. DREVER and R. JOHNSTON. The Petrology of Picritic Rocks in Minor Intrusions—A Hebridean Group. *Trans. Roy. Soc. Edin.*, vol. lxiii, pp. 459–499.

1961. P. J. WYLLIE. Fusion of Torridonian Sandstone by a Picritic Sill in Soay, (Hebrides). *Journ. Petrology*, vol. 2, pp. 1–37.

1962. L. R. WAGER and E. A. VINCENT. Ferrodiorite from the Isle of Skye. *Mineralogical Mag.*, vol. 33, pp. 22–36.

VII. LATE TERTIARY, PLEISTOCENE AND RECENT

1. LATE TERTIARY EROSION

IMPRESSIVE EVIDENCE OF the extent of late Tertiary erosion is afforded by the Inner Hebrides. The Tertiary lava-plateau has been dissected into mere remnants, and the volcanoes, marked by the local vents and intrusions, have been laid bare to their roots. Plutonic masses which must have consolidated under a considerable cover have been partly or wholly de-roofed. Much the greater part of this erosion is concluded to have been effected prior to the Pleistocene period.

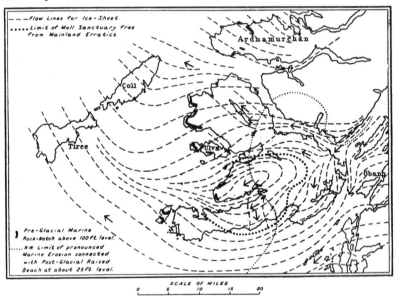

FIG. 57. *General Glaciation Map of the Mull–Ardnamurchan Region, and some Raised-beach Phenomena*

[Rep. from *Tertiary Mull Memoir*, 1924, Fig. 65]

In the Inner Hebrides and Arran there are relics of the well-known platforms recognized in Scotland, which have been ascribed to marine denudation and base levelling. The many peaks attaining to 2,000 and even 3,000 ft. in Mull, Skye and Arran suggest that the Tertiary igneous rocks were involved in the formation of the 2,000 to 3,000-ft. platform of the Highlands. This plane of marine denudation, or base levelling, is therefore dated as later than the Tertiary igneous period. Another platform at or about 1,000 or 1,200 ft. is known in Arran (1911, 1914)* and elsewhere, and includes the Lorne Plateau on the mainland opposite Mull. It is supposed to be of Pliocene age. The continental shelf, extending out to the 100-fathom line, forms a third platform of marine erosion. A fourth is well preserved as a wide rock-notch at some 120 to 150 ft. above the O.D. along the north-west side of Mull, in the adjoining Treshnish Isles and in Ardnamurchan. It is likely that this platform was cut not long prior to the Pleistocene period (1911a, 1924, 1930).

* Dates within brackets refer to References on p. 116.

2. PLEISTOCENE AND RECENT

In Pleistocene times a great ice-sheet moved westwards from the Highlands-over the Hebridean region towards the Atlantic. Striae, roches moutonnées and carried-boulders mark its course. Boulder clay is usually patchy, having accumulated mainly in sheltered places, and is sometimes absent over entire districts. The more mountainous areas, such as Northern Arran, Central Mull and Central Skye, bore their own local ice-cap; and within the limits of the ice-pressure from their own mountains no boulders from the Scottish mainland are found.

The final stage of local glaciation is marked by moundy moraines in districts such as Mull, Skye, Arran and St. Kilda, and sometimes by crescentic moraines, as well as by striae along the sides of the valleys. U-shaped valleys and corries are also typical of the mountainous areas. In Skye the striated rock-basin of Loch Coruisk bears striking witness to the downward-eroding capacity of a valley glacier (p. 4). In St. Kilda, L. R. Wager has recently found evidence of minor local glaciation, including the moraine of a small valley glacier at Village Bay; it seems clear, however, that the mainland ice-sheet that extended over the Outer Hebrides did not reach the island (1953).

A. Harker made a comprehensive analysis of the glaciation of Skye (1901); here the causes of cirque formation have been reconsidered (1938). The physiographic evolution and glaciation of Arran have been studied in detail by F. Mort and G. W. Tyrrell (1911, 1914, 1928). The glaciation of Mull, Ardnamurchan and the Small Isles has been dealt with in Geological Survey memoirs. Recently J. K. Charlesworth has published a synthesis of the Late-Glacial history of the Highlands and Islands (1956). The late-stage valley glaciers of Arran, Mull, Rum and Skye are assigned to his Moraine Glaciation, a stage of his more extensive Highland Glaciation. The Moraine Glaciation is correlated with the 100-ft. raised beach. Individual valley glaciers of the Tertiary volcanic centres are assigned to various sub-stages of the Moraine Glaciation, but these correlations are based on considerations of height and probable snowline and are admittedly hypothetical.

In Mull (1924), valley glaciers did not retreat until the sea stood at less than 100 ft. above its present level. In Glen Forsa, eskers and outwash fans are well developed below this height, and there are no beach deposits of the 100-ft. Late-Glacial sea. The deposits of the 100-ft. raised beach extend into the seaward parts of many other valleys in Mull, and indeed throughout the Tertiary region, but the beach is nowhere marked by any pronounced rock-notch (1928a). In contrast, the deposits of the Post-Glacial 25-ft. raised beach lie upon a wide platform in the Central Mull-Oban area. Farther north this feature becomes less well developed, but it forms a practically continuous shelf around the island of Arran.

Wherever the Tertiary lavas rest on Jurassic rocks landslipping tends to occur. In the Trotternish peninsula of Skye the eastern lava scarp reaches, in places, over 2,000 ft. and the landslip area assumes impressive proportions (1935-40), extending for some 14 miles from Beinn a' Chearcaill in the south to Meall na Suiramach in the north, with a maximum width of $1\frac{1}{2}$ miles at the Quiraing, west of Staffin Bay. Other spectacular examples are on the eastern side of Ben Tianavaig, near Portree, at Score Horan in Vaternish and on the eastern side of Dun Caan in Raasay. The Jurassic sediments are the incompetent strata and the sole of the slip is invariably in these rocks. The collapse of the overriding basalt lavas has given the Trotternish landslip area its characteristic topography: ridges of chaotically-tilted blocks which weather down to rugged pinnacles, of which the Old Man of Storr is an example. Small lochans, sometimes containing diatomite (p. 117), have formed between the ridges, where peat is also extensively developed. Although slipping must have been initiated by the formation of Tertiary fault scarps, the earlier slipped material was removed during the Pleistocene glaciation. With the retreat of the ice, landslipping again developed and has continued to the present day.

Deposits of recent date include peat, river alluvium, blown sand, often with much comminuted shelly material, and diatomaceous earth (Skye and Mull). Olivine-sands, derived from picritic dolerite sills, have accumulated locally on the shores of Northern Skye and Southern Raasay (1930a, 1935). In Skye, sand formed of the broken stems of the nullipore *Lithothamnion calcareum* forms gleaming white beaches near Claigan, north of Dunvegan (1939).

REFERENCES

1901. A. HARKER. Ice-erosion in the Cuillin Hills, Skye. *Trans. Roy. Soc. Edin.*, vol. xl, pt. ii, pp. 221–252.

1911. F. MORT. The Sculpture of the Goat Fell Mountain Group. *Scottish Geogr. Mag.*, vol. xxvii, pp. 632–643.

1911a. W. B. WRIGHT. On a Pre-Glacial Shore-line in the Western Isles of Scotland. *Geol. Mag.*, dec. v, vol. viii, pp. 97–104.

1914. F. MORT. The Sculpture of North Arran. *Scottish Geogr. Mag.*, vol. xxx, pp. 393–404.

1924. E. B. BAILEY and others. The Tertiary and Post-Tertiary Geology of Mull, Loch Aline and Oban. *Mem. Geol. Surv.*

1928. G. W. TYRRELL. The Geology of Arran. *Mem. Geol. Surv.*

1928a. W. B. WRIGHT. The Raised Beaches of the British Isles. In *First Report of the Commission on Pliocene and Pleistocene Terraces. (International Geographical Union)*. Oxford. (pp. 99–106).

1930. J. E. RICHEY, H. H. THOMAS and others. The Geology of Ardnamurchan, North-west Mull and Coll. *Mem. Geol. Surv.*

1930a. F. WALKER. An Olivine Sand from Duntulm, Skye. *Trans. Edin. Geol. Soc.*, vol. xii, pt. iii, pp. 321–322.

1935. C. F. DAVIDSON. The Tertiary Geology of Raasay, Inner Hebrides. *Trans. Roy. Soc. Edin.*, vol. lviii, pt. ii, pp. 375–407.

1935–40. G. V. WILSON and others. *In* Summaries of Progress of the Geological Survey (*Mems. Geol. Surv.*): for 1934, pt. I, pp. 70–71; for 1935, pt. I, pp. 81–84; for 1936, pt. I, pp. 77–79; for 1937, pp. 73–74; for 1938, pp. 74–76.

1938. W. V. LEWIS. A Melt-water Hypothesis of Cirque Formation. *Geol. Mag.*, vol. lxxv, pp. 249–265.

1939. D. HALDANE. Note on the Nullipore or Coralline Sand of Dunvegan, Skye. *Trans. Edin. Geol. Soc.*, vol. xiii, pt. iv, pp. 442–444.

1953. L. R. WAGER. The Extent of Glaciation in the Island of St. Kilda. *Geol. Mag.*, vol. xc, pp. 177–181.

1956. J. K. CHARLESWORTH. The Late-Glacial History of the Highlands and Islands of Scotland. *Trans. Roy. Soc. Edin.*, vol. lxii, pt. iii, pp. 769–928. (Tertiary Districts, pp. 874–881, 884–885, 917, 921–922).

See also list of Geological Survey Memoirs on p. 120: North Arran etc.; West-Central Skye; Small Isles of Inverness-shire; Glenelg, Lochalsh and S.E. Skye; Staffa, Iona and W. Mull.

VIII. MINERAL DEPOSITS

THE TERTIARY REGION is comparatively poor in raw materials of industrial value at the present day. The more important deposits are listed below in alphabetical order, with brief notes on their characters and on their past and current exploitation.

Barytes. Veins of good quality barytes were mined in Glen Sannox, Arran, from 1836 to 1862 and from 1918 until about 1939, when the workings became unproductive. Later exploration did not lead to renewal of mining (1928, 1944).*

Building Stone. In Arran, red Permian sandstone near Lamlash, Brodick and Corrie and white Carboniferous sandstone near Corrie have, in the past, been extensively quarried for building purposes. The thick acid and basic sills of Arran have also provided building stone (1909, 1928). In Skye, Jurassic free-stones were formerly exploited near Broadford and Torridonian grits in Sleat (1910).

The pink granite of the Ross of Mull was once extensively quarried for use in the construction of lighthouses, bridges and quays; it is a very sound stone and can be obtained in large blocks. Ross of Mull granite is incorporated in the fabric of Iona Cathedral, but the stone used may have been derived from glacial erratics (1925, 1925a).

Diatomite. Diatomite (kieselguhr) was worked at Loch Cuithir and at Sartil in Northern Skye between 1899 and 1914; exploitation was renewed at Loch Cuithir shortly after the 1939-45 war. Diatomite also occurs at one or two other localities in Northern Skye (1887, 1940a). In Mull, near Knock at the north end of Loch Bà (1924, 1940a), and on Eigg (1940a) diatomite deposits are also known.

Iron Ore. An oolitic limy ironstone in the Upper Lias of Raasay (p. 30 and Fig. 13) is the only iron ore that has been worked. The bed has an average thickness of 8 ft. and was mined intensively during the war of 1914–18. Two varieties of ironstone occur, one rich in ooliths set in a limestone matrix, the other with sparse ooliths set in a dark irony matrix. The iron is mainly in the form of a green mineral, chamosite (hydrous silicate of iron, magnesia and alumina), but in the darker variety iron oxides are developed and apparently also some siderite. The average mined rock yielded 23 to 25 per cent of iron and 22 per cent of lime. The probable reserves were estimated in 1940 at 10,000,000 tons. An investigation of the future potentialities of the field was undertaken in 1959 by a Scottish steel manufacturing firm. No workable ironstone is known elsewhere in the Jurassic rocks of Scotland (1914, 1920, 1920a, 1940).

Magnetite occurs in Skye as a contact-metasomatic deposit in Durness Limestone at the margin of the Beinn an Dubhaich Granite (p. 92). During the last war and in 1947 magnetometer surveys indicated the presence of iron ore at 27 localities, along the granite margin and in enclaves of limestone within the granite. The aggregate quantity of ore estimated to be present at shallow depth at two localities was between 32,000 and 37,000 tons. The ore contains copper and would be difficult to work; for these reasons the wartime investigation did not lead to exploitation (1949a, 1951, 1952, 1952a).

* Dates within brackets refer to References on p. 119.

117

Lignite and Coal. Coal of poor quality was worked in the late 18th century in the Carboniferous Limestone Series near the Cock of Arran; the occurrence has no economic value to-day (1928).

Thin lenticular seams of lignite (or brown coal) occur locally below, or intercalated in, the Tertiary lavas of South-west Mull, Skye, Ardnamurchan and Canna. The lignites of South-west Mull and Skye have been wrought to some extent at the outcrop for local domestic use or for blacksmith's work. The seams attain a thickness of between 2 and 3 ft. only locally, and are mostly much thinner; they have a high content of ash and are not of economic value. Thin impure coals of no economic interest also occur in the Jurassic strata of North-east Skye (1920*a*, 1922, 1925, 1925*a*, 1930).

Limestone. Limestones of various ages have been quarried locally in all districts for burning in kilns. Carboniferous limestone of high purity was quarried in Arran during the war of 1914–18. Limestones and dolomites of the Durness Limestones of Skye have been sampled and studied petrographically and chemically in relation to industrial use in the steel-making industry, but the investigation has not led to exploitation (1928, 1949, 1954, 1956).

Marble. In Strath, Skye, contact-metamorphism due to granite and gabbro has locally converted Durness Limestone into marble, dolomitic beds giving rise to forsterite- and brucite-marbles (p. 92). These marbles, some pure white in colour, have been quarried at intervals during the last 150 years for ornamental purposes, including terrazzo work; they are not now exploited (1904, 1910, 1949, 1954, 1956).

Oil-Shale. A bed of oil-shale, 8 to 10 ft. thick, occurs at the base of the Great Estuarine Series in Raasay (Fig. 13). Tests of samples have indicated a yield of 12 gallons of crude oil, and 6·2 lb. of sulphate of ammonia, per ton of shale. The samples tested were much weathered and somewhat higher yields of oil might possibly be given by fresh shale. An oil-shale with a test yield up to 17 gallons of crude oil per ton is known at the same horizon on the north-east coast of Skye, in the neighbourhood of Portree. Neither occurrence is of economic value at the present day (1920*a*, 1922).

Sand and Silica-Rock. Sandstones suitable for various industrial purposes (moulding, hearth and glass sands) occur in the Carboniferous, Permian and Triassic rocks of Arran (1909, 1928, 1945).

The Upper Cretaceous Sandstone of Lochaline, Morvern, is exceptionally pure (silica up to 99·69 per cent). Since 1941 this soft 20-ft. bed, which lies close below the Tertiary lavas, has been mined as a source of glass sand. The highest grade material provides a first-class sand for use in the manufacture of optical glass; the remainder is used for bottle-making and for glassware of various kinds (1925, 1945).

Cambrian quartzite at Ord, Skye, has for some years been quarried by a manufacturer of refractory products (1945).

Sapphire. In xenoliths enclosed in sills around Loch Scridain in Mull (Fig. 33), and in a mass of altered rock at Glebe Hill, near Kilchoan, in Ardnamurchan, sapphires are plentiful. In Mull, the crystals are sometimes as much as an inch across, but they are thin and full of inclusions. It is unlikely that there are any crystals of commercial value (1924, 1925*a*, 1930).

REFERENCES

1887. J. S. G. WILSON and W. I. MACADAM. Diatomaceous Deposits in Skye. *Trans. Edin. Geol. Soc.*, vol. v, pt. ii, pp. 318–326.

1904. A. HARKER. The Tertiary Igneous Rocks of Skye. *Mem. Geol. Surv.*

1909. R. BOYLE. The Economic and Petrographic Geology of the New Red Sandstones of the South and West of Scotland. *Trans. Geol. Soc. Glasgow*, vol. xiii, pt. iii, pp. 344–384.

1910. C. T. CLOUGH and others. The Geology of Glenelg, Lochalsh and South-East Part of Skye. *Mem. Geol. Surv.*

1914. W. THORNEYCROFT. Note on the Upper Lias of the Western Islands in reference to the Iron Ore Deposit therein. *Trans. Edin. Geol. Soc.*, vol. x, pt. ii, pp. 196–204.

1920. M. MACGREGOR and others. The Iron Ores of Scotland. *Spec. Rep. Min. Res. Gt. Brit.*, vol. xi, *Mem. Geol. Surv.*

1920a. G. W. LEE. The Mesozoic Rocks of Applecross, Raasay and North-East Skye. *Mem. Geol. Surv.*

1922. W. GIBSON. Cannel Coals, Lignite and Mineral Oil in Scotland. *Spec. Rep. Min. Res. Gt. Brit.*, vol. xxiv. *Mem. Geol. Surv.*

1924. E. B. BAILEY and others. The Tertiary and Post-Tertiary Geology of Mull, Loch Aline and Oban. *Mem. Geol. Surv.*

1925. G. W. LEE and E. B. BAILEY. The Pre-Tertiary Geology of Mull, Loch Aline and Oban. *Mem. Geol. Surv.*

1925a. E. B. BAILEY and E. M. ANDERSON. The Geology of Staffa, Iona and Western Mull. *Mem. Geol. Surv.*

1928. G. W. TYRRELL. The Geology of Arran. *Mem. Geol. Surv.*

1930. J. E. RICHEY and H. H. THOMAS. The Geology of Ardnamurchan, North-West Mull and Coll. *Mem. Geol. Surv.*

1940. M. MACGREGOR and others. Synopsis of the Mineral Resources of Scotland. *Spec. Rep. Min. Res. Gt. Brit.*, vol. xxxiii. *Mem. Geol. Surv.*

1940a. D. HALDANE and others. Diatomite. *Wartime Pamphlet of the Geological Survey*, No. 5.

1944. A. G. MACGREGOR and M. MACGREGOR. Barytes in Central Scotland. *Wartime Pamphlet of the Geological Survey*, No. 38.

1945. J. G. C. ANDERSON. High-Grade Silica Rocks of the Scottish Highlands and Islands. *Wartime Pamphlet of the Geological Survey*, No. 7, Second Ed.

1949. T. ROBERTSON and others. The Limestones of Scotland. *Spec. Rep. Min. Res. Gt. Brit.*, vol. xxxv. *Mem. Geol. Surv.*

1949a. *Report of the Mineral Development Committee* (Ministry of Fuel and Power). London. H.M. Stationery Office.

1951. J. T. WHETTON and J. O. MYERS. Geophysical Survey of Magnetite Deposits in Strath, Skye. *Trans. Geol. Soc. Glas.*, vol. xxi, pt. ii, pp. 263–277.

1952. A. W. GROVES. Wartime Investigations into the Haematite and Manganese Ore Resources of Gt. Britain and Northern Ireland. *Min. of Supply Permanent Records of Research and Development*. Monograph 20–703.

1952a. T. H. WHITEHEAD. Some Magnetite Ores in Scotland: (a) Strath, Skye (Inverness-shire). *Internat. Geol. Congress, 19th Session, Algiers 1952. Symposium sur les Gisements de Fer du Monde*, vol. II, pp. 417–419.

1954. H. E. WILSON. Cambro-Ordovician Limestones and Dolomites of the Ord and Torran areas, Skye and the Kishorn area, Ross-shire. *Spec. Rep. Min. Res. Gt. Brit.*, vol. xxxvi. *Mem. Geol. Surv.*

1956. A. MUIR, J. PHEMISTER and others. The Limestones of Scotland: Chemical Analyses and Petrography. *Spec. Rep. Min. Res. Gt. Brit.*, vol. xxxvii. *Mem. Geol. Surv.*

IX. GEOLOGICAL SURVEY MEMOIRS DEALING WITH THE TERTIARY VOLCANIC DISTRICTS

(For Economic Memoirs and Pamphlets, see p. 119)

1903. The Geology of North Arran, South Bute and the Cumbraes, with Parts of Ayrshire and Kintyre.

1904. The Geology of West-Central Skye, with Soay.

1904. The Tertiary Igneous Rocks of Skye.

1908. The Geology of the Small Isles of Inverness-shire (Rum, Canna, Eigg, Muck, etc.).

1910. The Geology of Glenelg, Lochalsh and South-East Part of Skye.

1911. The Geology of Colonsay and Oronsay, with Part of the Ross of Mull.

1920. The Mesozoic Rocks of Applecross, Raasay and North-East Skye.

1924. The Tertiary and Post-Tertiary Geology of Mull, Loch Aline and Oban.

1925. The Pre-Tertiary Geology of Mull, Loch Aline and Oban.

1925. The Geology of Staffa, Iona and Western Mull.

1928. The Geology of Arran.

1930. The Geology of Ardnamurchan, North-West Mull and Coll.

1931. Chemical Analyses of Igneous Rocks, Metamorphic Rocks and Minerals.

1934. Guide to the Geological Model of Ardnamurchan.

1956. Chemical Analyses of Igneous Rocks, Metamorphic Rocks and Minerals: 1931–1954.

Most of the above publications are out of print

Printed in Scotland for Her Majesty's Stationery Office
by H. K. Clarkson & Son Ltd., Dd 020102 K56 1/76.